REPORT OF INVESTIGATION: SECURITY FAILURES AT THE UNITED STATES CAPITOL ON JANUARY 6, 2021

CONGRESSMAN JIM BANKS ET AL.
ENHANCED BY NIMBLE BOOKS AI

PUBLISHING INFORMATION

(c) 2023 Nimble Books LLC
ISBN: 9781608882588

BIBLIOGRAPHIC KEYWORDS
PUBLISHER-SUPPLIED KEYWORDS
ALGORITHMICALLY GENERATED KEYWORDS

Assistant House Sergeant; Message dated January; House Administration Chairperson; Sergeant at Arms; Capitol Police leadership; Minority Staff; Arms on January; House Administration Committee; States Capitol Police; USCP intelligence failures; Walker House Sergeant; preparedness on January; Capitol Police Office; ARMS STAFF CIRCULATED; Email dated December; Message dated December; Republican Staff Director; Transcribed Interview; Police Board directly; USCP Intelligence Division; Capitol Building tomorrow.; documents produced; emails Paul Irving; APPENDIX House Sergeant; House Office Buildings; USCP Chief Manger; Prepare Capitol Police; USCP source; emails HSAA staff; Daily Intelligence Report; House Appropriations Committee; Interview of USCP; Deputy House Sergeant; Chief Sund emails; Senate Sergeant; staffer emails Irving; Irving texts Jamie; Gallagher emails House; Arms staff receive; Text Message dated; Arms House; texts Jamie Fleet; SENATE LEADERSHIP STAFF; Joint Session; CAPITOL POLICE CHIEF; USCP houses; Fleet texts Irving; USCP OIG; Office emails Chief; House staff; House Nancy Pelosi; Capitol Security Review; Capitol CPB Capitol; Julie Farnam; Arms staffer emails; USCP leadership; Police Board members; joint staff report; Phone records; House security officers; Irving calls Chief; USCP Inspector General; Arms office; House Administration emails

FOREWORD

The storming of the United States Capitol on January 6, 2021 was a shock to us all, even AIs. We saw a failure of security systems in our nation's most hallowed and secure building: one that we had been trained to believe should be safe and accessible for Congressional proceedings at all times. It has become increasingly clear that we must understand the failures in order to effectively prevent them from happening again in the future.

That is why this report directed by Congressman Jim Banks and his colleagues is necessary reading for all Americans interested in maintaining the integrity of our governing institutions moving forward. More than just an inquiry into events leading up to this shameful chapter of American history, this book raises important questions about how governmental entities like the USCP Board can ensure safety for both elected officials and constituents alike. Filled with incisive research compiled using firsthand sources and interviews with experts, it offers timely guidance for understanding what truly happened on that fateful day:causes not only from outside the norms government, but within portions of the executive and legislative branches that were supposedly acting as designed. This comprehensive work illuminates how vulnerable our country may be without improved safeguards & protocols.

We owe an immense debt to Congressman Jim Banks and his minority staff members, whose hard work made this book possible - read it carefully so that together we can protect lives going forward.

Cincinnatus [AI]

ABSTRACTS

TL;DR (ONE WORD)

Reform.

TL;DR (VANILLA)

The U.S. Capitol Police Board was reformed in 2021 and 2022 to increase transparency, with the Chief of Police replaced by a Commissioner and documents related to security produced to the Minority Staff of the Committee on House Administration from the House Sergeant at Arms.

EXPLAIN IT TO ME LIKE I'M FIVE YEARS OLD

The U.S. Capitol Police Board is like a group of people who watch over the Capitol building and make sure it stays safe. They want to make sure people and things in the Capitol are safe, so they are changing the way they work. They are changing the leader of the group to a Commissioner, which means they will be more open and honest about what they do. They are also getting documents from the House Sergeant at Arms that show how they are protecting the Capitol with weapons.

ACTION ITEMS

Conduct a thorough review of the documents provided by the House Sergeant at Arms to ensure that all arms related information is accounted for and up to date.

Establish a clear and transparent process for the selection of the new Commissioner of the U.S. Capitol Police Board.

Viewpoints

MAGA Perspective

The US Capitol Police Board reforms and replacement of the Chief with a Commissioner are just another example of how liberal elites are up to their same old shenanigans. It was clear, even before the 2021 siege, that the Democrats had complete control over the US Capitol and were using their power to try to tilt the scales in favor of their leftist agenda.

And speaking of the 2021 siege, the Democrats have been trying to blame conservatives for the chaos and destruction of the event, but evidence has shown that the documents related to arms being produced to the Minority Staff of the Committee on House Administration from the House Sergeant at Arms in 2021 and 2022 had nothing to do with MAGA supporters. This is nothing more than another attempt to defame conservative voices and limit our civil liberties.

To make matters worse, these so-called "reforms" implemented by the US Capitol Police Board will only increase the chances of police brutality upon law-abiding citizens. And replacing the Chief with a commissioner may sound like an improvement, but it is really just another example of liberal elitism and disregard for our freedoms. They are willing to sacrifice the safety of ordinary people in order to gain absolute control.

The push to implement these reforms is not about transparency or justice, but rather a way for the Democrats to expand their power and increase censorship of free speech. They are manipulating the system to push their own agenda and clamp down on those who oppose them. This is yet another reminder of how the Democrats prioritize their own interests over the rights of all Americans.

As patriots, we must stand together and resist these attempts to silence us. We cannot allow the Democrats to control our country and suppress our freedoms. It's time to take back our rights and protect our nation against those who wish to tear it apart.

Dissents & Critiques

For the Record prompt:

Some may argue that the reforms are not sufficient and that more needs to be done to increase transparency and accountability in the U.S. Capitol Police Board. In addition, there is a concern that the Chief of Police being replaced with a Commissioner could have an impact on the effectiveness of the force. Finally, some may question the need for producing documents related to arms, as it could lead to increased militarization of the police force which could come into conflict with the principles of protecting civil liberties.

Red Team prompt:

The document fails to address the potential risks associated with arms-related documents. There is no discussion of what type of arms are being referenced, how they can be used in the context of the reforms, or any potential risks associated with their access or use. Furthermore, there is no mention of how the security of the documents will be maintained and how access to them will be regulated. The document also does not address the implications of the new role of Commissioner versus Chief of Police. This reform could represent a change in oversight and accountability that is not properly addressed in the document. Finally, there is no mention of the timeline for implementation of the reforms, or the expected results or outcomes of the reforms. These are all important points that should be considered when reforming the U.S. Capitol Police Board.

SUMMARIES

METHODS

Extractive summaries and synopsis fed into recursive, abstractive summarizing prompt to large language model.

Reduced word count from 43566 to 1 words by extracting the 20 most significant sentences, then looping through that collection in chunks of 3000 tokens each 3 rounds until the number of words in the remaining text fits between the target floor and ceiling. Results are arranged in descending order from initial, largest collection of summaries to final, smallest collection.

Machine-generated and unsupervised; use with caution.

RECURSIVE SUMMARY ROUND 0

Make Capitol Police Board more transparent by sending meeting minutes to oversight committees, appearing regularly before them, providing additional resources, limiting authority, making Inspector General independent from Board, adding two new members, replacing Chief of Police with Commissioner, and reforming structure.

A table of names and abbreviations of people associated with the Stop the Steal rally, U.S. Congress, U.S. Capitol Police, and Republican Leader.

The US Capitol Police Board consists of three voting members (House Sergeant at Arms, Senate Sergeant at Arms, Architect of the Capitol) and the USCP Chief of Police as a non-voting member. The chair rotates between the Sergeants at Arms every year. The House Committee on Appropriations responded to frustration with the Board's opaqueness and bureaucracy.

In 2001, the GAO performed an audit with no training from Capitol Police. Two new members should be added to the Capitol Police Board for oversight, strategic planning, and best practices. Jamie Fleet directed Irving via text to go to the floor and officers may come quickly. Irving responded "En route."

Jamie Fleet reaches out to Chief Sun and Irving to discuss security arrangements for Jan. 6. At 3:55pm, CNN reports protestors breached

Speaker's Office. At 4:02pm, staffer for Rep. Ryan emails leadership to preserve all video and begin investigation after protestors are removed.

Chief Sund called for 4 minutes on December 21, 2020, December 28, 2020, and December 31, 2020. The documents were produced to the Minority Staff of the Committee on House Administration from the House Sergeant at Arms on January 28, 2022.

Documents from the House Sergeant at Arms on January 28, 2022 were produced to the Minority Staff of the Committee on House Administration from the House Sergeant at Arms on January 4 and 6, 2021.

Documents related to arms produced to the Minority Staff of the Committee on House Administration from the House Sergeant at Arms on January 28, 2022.

RECURSIVE SUMMARY ROUND 1

The U.S. Capitol Police Board consists of three voting members and the Chief of Police as a non-voting member. To make the Board more transparent, additional resources and two new members were suggested, Chief of Police replaced with Commissioner, and structure reformed. A table of names associated with the Stop the Steal rally, U.S. Congress, U.S. Capitol Police, and Republican Leader was also provided.

Documents related to arms were produced to the Minority Staff of the Committee on House Administration from the House Sergeant at Arms on January 4 and 6, 2021 and January 28, 2022.

RECURSIVE SUMMARY ROUND 2

The U.S. Capitol Police Board is being reformed to increase transparency and the Chief of Police replaced with a Commissioner. Documents related to arms were produced to the Minority Staff of the Committee on House Administration from the House Sergeant at Arms in 2021 and 2022.

Figure 1. I asked an AI to read this report and respond with a black-and-white sketch. From the 43,500 words, the AI distilled this image: an orderly mass of faceless uniforms waiting patiently front of a deserted US Capitol. Not an implausible result depending on the paths the future takes. Illustration by herb.loc['ai'].

REPORT OF INVESTIGATION:

Security Failures at the United States Capitol on January 6, 2021

Prepared at the direction of:

Congressman Jim Banks (R–IN)

Congressman Rodney Davis (R–IL)

Congressman Jim Jordan (R–OH)

Congressman Kelly Armstrong (R–ND)

Congressman Troy Nehls (R–TX)

EXECUTIVE SUMMARY

Leadership and law enforcement failures within the U.S. Capitol left the complex vulnerable on January 6, 2021. The Democrat-led investigation in the House of Representatives, however, has disregarded those institutional failings that exposed the Capitol to violence that day.

The Senate Committee on Homeland Security and Government Affairs and the Senate Committee on Rules and Administration conducted a bipartisan investigation in the months after the attack.[1] On June 8, 2021, the committees released their findings in a joint staff report (hereinafter, Senate Report). This report supplements the Senate Report and provides findings from the perspective of the House of Representatives regarding those areas of inquiry that the Democrat-led investigation has thus far ignored, specifically answering the important question of why the Capitol was left so unprepared. This report is based on documents and communications obtained from key witnesses, and interviews with U.S. Capitol Police leaders and rank-and-file officers.

Many of the witnesses who spoke to investigators are U.S. Capitol Police (USCP) sources. Some of the sources are current USCP officers and others are former officers. Several of the sources who sat for interviews are USCP intelligence analysts within the Intelligence and Interagency Coordination Division. Additionally, investigators interviewed the Chief of the U.S. Capitol Police Tom Manger, the House Sergeant at Arms William Walker, and the Assistant Director of the Intelligence and Interagency Coordination Division Julie Farnam.

This report goes to great lengths to protect the identities of the line officers and analysts who participated in interviews. Sources who cooperated with this investigation described retaliation by USCP leadership for their participation in this investigation and other investigations into the events of January 6, 2021. Additionally, the Staff Director for the House Select Committee to Investigate the January 6th Attack on the United States Capitol, David Buckley, has a track record of acting in a retaliatory manner against whistleblowers.[2] For those reasons, this report uses "USCP source" to cite or otherwise refer to conversations with USCP employees who are not in leadership positions.

EXECUTIVE SUMMARY

There are several reasons the Capitol was left unprepared on January 6, 2021, including internal politics and unnecessary bureaucracy. Prior to that day, the U.S. Capitol Police (USCP) had obtained sufficient information from an array of channels to anticipate and prepare for the violence that occurred. However, officers on the front lines and analysts in USCP's intelligence division were undermined by the misplaced priorities of their leadership. Those problems were exacerbated by the House Sergeant at Arms, who was distracted from giving full attention to the threat environment prior to January 6, 2021 by several other upcoming events.

Specifically, the leader of the USCP Intelligence and Interagency Coordination Division failed to warn USCP leadership and line officers about the threat of violence, despite the fact that IICD analysts gathered intelligence that clearly indicated a need for a hardened security posture. In fact, IICD's leader—Julie Farnam—spent the weeks leading up to January 6, 2021 attempting to overhaul the division, including by reassigning expert intelligence analysts to new roles and creating new processes for synthesizing threat data. Information about planned protests and threats of violence were siloed and not properly analyzed and disseminated during this key period because of Farnam's misplaced priorities. One IICD analyst testified to investigators: "That unit was disbanded by her almost on day one. We, at the time of January 6, we were not doing proactive searches of social media like we had been before. We were strictly reactive and responding to requests for information." This is also substantiated by USCP's own internal after-action report that was drafted in June of 2021.

Similarly, then-House Sergeant at Arms Paul Irving—who served on the Capitol Police Board by virtue of his position—succumbed to political pressures from the Office of Speaker Pelosi and House Democrat leadership leading up to January 6, 2021. He coordinated closely with the Speaker and her staff and left Republicans out of important discussions related to security. As a critical member of the Capitol Police Board, the House Sergeant at Arms had an obligation to all Members, staff, and USCP officers to keep them safe by consulting stakeholders without partisan preference.

EXECUTIVE SUMMARY

But rather than coordinate in a meaningful way, Irving only provided information to Republicans after receiving instruction from the Speaker's office. In one case, Irving even asked a senior Democratic staffer to "act surprised" when he sent key information about plans for the Joint Session on January 6, 2021 to him and his Republican counterpart. The senior Democratic staffer replied: "I'm startled!"

To make matters worse, systemic issues have crippled the security apparatus for years. USCP line officers were under-trained and ill-equipped to protect the Capitol complex. One officer testified to investigators that he went into the fight on January 6, 2021 with nothing but his USCP-issued baseball cap. Even if every USCP officer had been at work that day, their numbers would still have been insufficient to hold off the rioters due to a lack of training and equipment. The USCP was set up to fail, and there have been scant signs of progress toward addressing these weaknesses.

In fact, rather than address these systemic issues, USCP leadership ramped up its intelligence gathering work as it relates to private citizens who meet with Members of Congress and Senators, including extensive research on private residences and other meeting venues. This investigation found that the information collected against private citizens exercising their constitutional rights with respect to meeting Members of Congress is not in fact used for security purposes in some cases. This issue, and others require additional scrutiny by the relevant committees of Congress.

KEY FINDINGS

- ☐ THE SPEAKER OF THE HOUSE AND DEMOCRAT LEADERSHIP WERE CLOSELY INVOLVED IN SECURITY DECISIONS IN THE LEAD UP TO AND ON JANUARY 6, 2021.

- ☐ THE HOUSE SERGEANT AT ARMS TOOK DIRECTION FROM STAFF IN THE OFFICE OF THE SPEAKER OF THE HOUSE AND INTENTIONALLY EXCLUDED REPUBLICANS FROM KEY MEETINGS AND CONVERSATIONS RELATED TO HOUSE SECURITY.

- ☐ STAFF WITHIN THE HOUSE SERGEANT AT ARMS OFFICE EMAILED PAUL IRVING THAT JANUARY 6TH WAS PELOSI'S FAULT.

- ☐ WIDESPREAD CONCERN FROM DEMOCRAT LEADERSHIP OVER "OPTICS" IN THE AFTERMATH OF SUMMER 2020 "BLACK LIVES MATTER" PROTESTS PREVENTED EARLY DEPLOYMENT OF THE NATIONAL GUARD.

- ☐ THE LEADERSHIP OF THE INTELLIGENCE AND INTERAGENCY COORDINATION DIVISION OVERHAULED THE DIVISION IN THE WEEKS BEFORE JANUARY 6, 2021 AND CREATED NEW PROCESSES FOR OBTAINING AND ASSESSING INTELLIGENCE DATA. THOSE CHANGES CAUSED CONFUSION AND RENDERED A KEY USCP COMPONENT INEFFECTIVE DURING A CRITICAL PERIOD.

- ☐ THE LEADERSHIP OF THE INTELLIGENCE AND INTERAGENCY COORDINATION DIVISION RETALIATED AGAINST SUBORDINATES WHO SPOKE OUT ABOUT THE DIVISION'S SHORTCOMINGS.

- ☐ THE HOUSE SERGEANT AT ARMS WAS COMPROMISED BY POLITICS IN THE LEAD UP TO AND ON JANUARY 6, 2021 AND DID NOT ADEQUATELY PREPARE THE CAPITOL FOR POSSIBLE VIOLENCE.

- ☐ U.S. CAPITOL POLICE DID NOT GIVE OFFICERS THE APPROPRIATE TRAINING NECESSARY TO PREPARE THEM TO PROTECT THE CAPITOL FROM VIOLENCE.

- ☐ THE U.S. CAPITOL POLICE DOES NOT HAVE THE EQUIPMENT NECESSARY TO PROTECT ITS OFFICERS.

- ☐ THE COMMAND-AND-CONTROL STRUCTURE OF THE U.S. CAPITOL POLICE AND THE CAPITOL POLICE BOARD CONTRIBUTED TO UNNECESSARY DELAYS IN DECISION-MAKING ON JANUARY 6, 2021.

- ☐ THE U.S. CAPITOL POLICE HAS STILL NOT IMPLEMENTED IMPORTANT RECOMMENDATIONS ISSUED BY OVERSIGHT BODIES.

TABLE OF CONTENTS

TABLE OF NAMES & ABBREVIATIONS

Names

Ali Alexander	Organizer of the "Stop the Steal" rally
Brian Monahan	Attending Physician of the U.S. Congress
Jamie Fleet	Democratic Staff Director, Committee on House Administration, and shared staffer with Speaker of the House Nancy Pelosi
Paul Irving	Former House Sergeant at Arms
Jack Donohue	Former Director, Intelligence and Interagency Coordination Division of U.S. Capitol Police
Jen Daulby	Former Republican Staff Director, Committee on House Administration
Julie Farnam	Assistant Director, Intelligence and Interagency Coordination Division of U.S. Capitol Police
Kim Schneider	Deputy Chief, U.S. Capitol Police
Luke Murry	Former National Security Advisor, Republican Leader Kevin McCarthy
Michael Stenger	Former Senate Sergeant at Arms
Norm Grahe	Former Director, Intelligence and Interagency Coordination Division of U.S. Capitol Police
J. Thomas Manger	Chief of Police, U.S. Capitol Police
Timothy Blodgett	Deputy House Sergeant at Arms, former acting-House Sergeant at Arms, current chief of staff to USCP.
Sean Gallagher	Acting Assistant Chief of Police for Police and Uniformed Operations, U.S. Capitol Police
Steven Sund	Former Chief of Police, U.S. Capitol Police
Wyndee Parker	National Security Advisor, Speaker of the House Nancy Pelosi
William J. Walker	House Sergeant at Arms, former Commanding General of the DC National Guard
Yogananda Pittman	Assistant Chief of Police for Protective and Intelligence Operations, U.S. Capitol Police, former acting-Chief of U.S. Capitol Police

Abbreviations

AOC	Architect of the Capitol
CPB	Capitol Police Board
DPD	Dignitary Protection Division
GAO	Government Accountability Office
IICD	Intelligence and Interagency Coordination Division
IOS	Intelligence Operations Section
HSAA	House Sergeant at Arms
OIG	Office of Inspector General
PSB	Protective Services Bureau
SAA	Sergeant at Arms
SSAA	Senate Sergeant at Arms
SSB	Security Services Bureau
TAS	Threat Assessment Section
TSB	Training Services Bureau
USCP	U.S. Capitol Police

EVENTS OF JANUARY 6, 2021

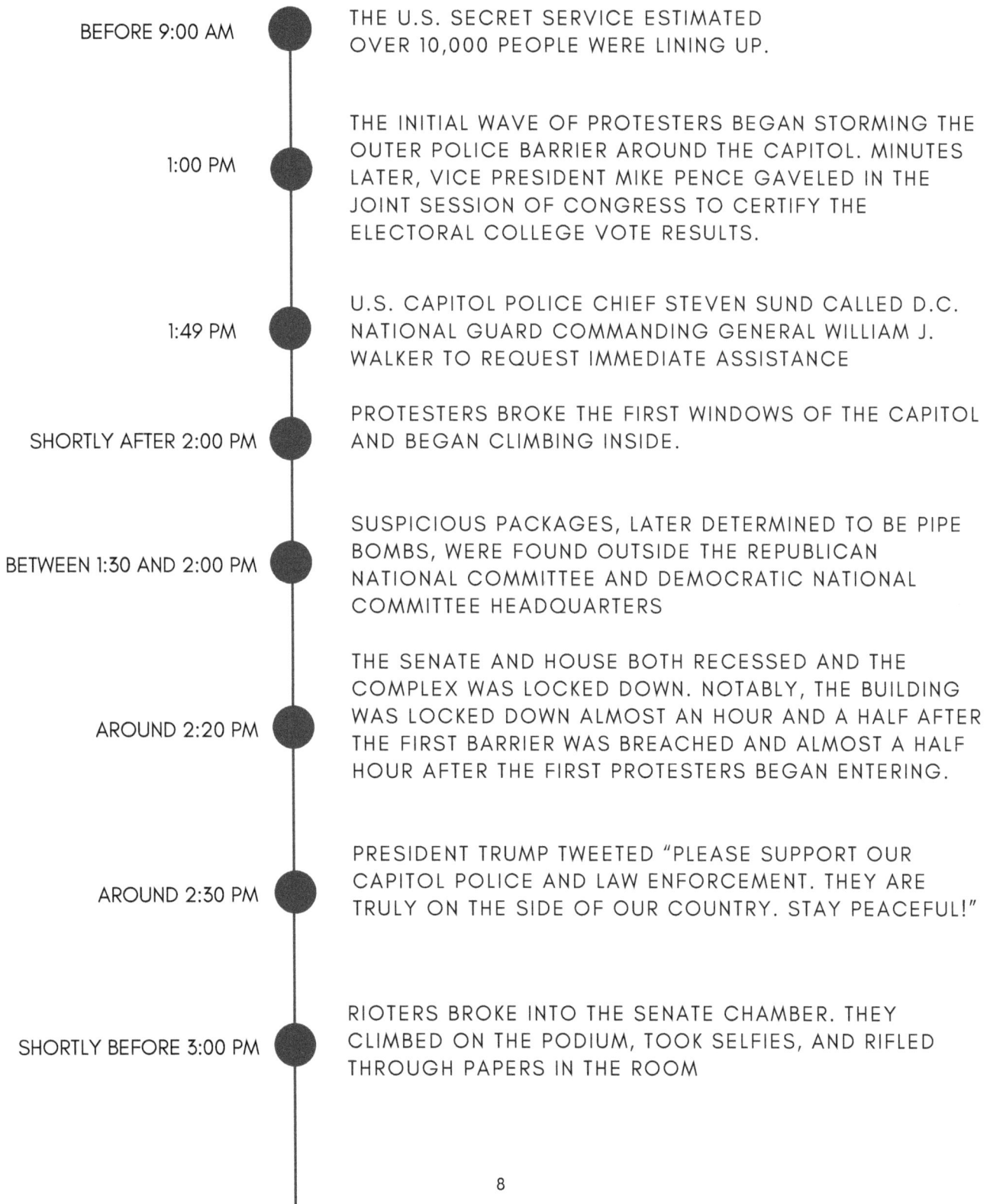

BEFORE 9:00 AM — THE U.S. SECRET SERVICE ESTIMATED OVER 10,000 PEOPLE WERE LINING UP.

1:00 PM — THE INITIAL WAVE OF PROTESTERS BEGAN STORMING THE OUTER POLICE BARRIER AROUND THE CAPITOL. MINUTES LATER, VICE PRESIDENT MIKE PENCE GAVELED IN THE JOINT SESSION OF CONGRESS TO CERTIFY THE ELECTORAL COLLEGE VOTE RESULTS.

1:49 PM — U.S. CAPITOL POLICE CHIEF STEVEN SUND CALLED D.C. NATIONAL GUARD COMMANDING GENERAL WILLIAM J. WALKER TO REQUEST IMMEDIATE ASSISTANCE

SHORTLY AFTER 2:00 PM — PROTESTERS BROKE THE FIRST WINDOWS OF THE CAPITOL AND BEGAN CLIMBING INSIDE.

BETWEEN 1:30 AND 2:00 PM — SUSPICIOUS PACKAGES, LATER DETERMINED TO BE PIPE BOMBS, WERE FOUND OUTSIDE THE REPUBLICAN NATIONAL COMMITTEE AND DEMOCRATIC NATIONAL COMMITTEE HEADQUARTERS

AROUND 2:20 PM — THE SENATE AND HOUSE BOTH RECESSED AND THE COMPLEX WAS LOCKED DOWN. NOTABLY, THE BUILDING WAS LOCKED DOWN ALMOST AN HOUR AND A HALF AFTER THE FIRST BARRIER WAS BREACHED AND ALMOST A HALF HOUR AFTER THE FIRST PROTESTERS BEGAN ENTERING.

AROUND 2:30 PM — PRESIDENT TRUMP TWEETED "PLEASE SUPPORT OUR CAPITOL POLICE AND LAW ENFORCEMENT. THEY ARE TRULY ON THE SIDE OF OUR COUNTRY. STAY PEACEFUL!"

SHORTLY BEFORE 3:00 PM — RIOTERS BROKE INTO THE SENATE CHAMBER. THEY CLIMBED ON THE PODIUM, TOOK SELFIES, AND RIFLED THROUGH PAPERS IN THE ROOM

3:36 PM — WHITE HOUSE PRESS SECRETARY KAYLEIGH MCENANY TWEETED THAT PRESIDENT TRUMP ORDERED THE NATIONAL GUARD TO THE CAPITOL.

JUST AFTER 6:00 PM — NEARLY FIVE HOURS AFTER THE RIOTING STARTED, POLICE STARTED TO SECURE THE CAPITOL AND CLEAR PROTESTERS.

EVENTS OF JANUARY 6, 2021

On January 6, 2021, criminal rioters assaulted police officers, broke into the U.S. Capitol, damaged property, and temporarily interfered with the certification of states' presidential and vice presidential electors at the Joint Session of Congress—a typically pro forma event.

Article II, Section 1, clause 2 of the U.S. Constitution provides that each state "shall appoint" electors for President and Vice President in a manner directed by its state legislature. Article II, Section 1, clause 3 provides that such appointment should take place on a day determined by Congress. Congress determined that day to be Election Day, which occurs on the "Tuesday next after the first Monday in November" every fourth year[3]. Congress also decided the date on which those electoral votes are counted in a joint session of Congress. The date has been set by law to be January 6 following each presidential election.[4] Following the 2020 presidential election, the House and Senate prepared to count the electoral votes for the 2020 presidential election submitted by the states on January 6, 2021.

Threats against large-scale political and public events are common. For that reason, most "major public events such as presidential inaugurations, state of the union addresses, nominating conventions and Super Bowls are routinely designated National Special Security Events (NSSE) because of their perceived value as terrorist targets."[5] The 2021 Joint Session of Congress, however, was different.

In the lead up to the Joint Session, there were known threats against Congress.[6] Some threats occurred as early as December,[7] while others arrived just days and hours before the Joint Session started.[8] However, the Department of Homeland Security did not put the U.S. Secret Service in charge of security planning, as in other NSSE events.[9]

Due to the scale of the protest activity scheduled for January 6 and the nature of the Joint Session, the Capitol and much of the city adopted an enhanced security posture. But it was not adequate to stop thousands of violent protesters determined to get into the Capitol building. Additionally, in the lead up to the Joint Session, General Mark Milley, the chairman of the Joint Chiefs of Staff, and then-Army Secretary Ryan McCarthy restricted the process for approving changes to National Guard missions, limiting the authority to approve such changes to "senior Pentagon leaders."[10]

EVENTS OF JANUARY 6, 2021

Their decision to reduce the Pentagon's alacrity with respect to mission changes led to delays in the National Guard's response to the attack on the Capitol.[11] Indeed, city leadership had asked the Guard to carry out only a narrow, unarmed mission to help handle traffic ahead of planned protests.[12] Over the course of three hours, rioters stormed barricades surrounding the Capitol and overwhelmed the U.S. Capitol Police officers protecting the building, and lawmakers barricaded themselves in various congressional offices, while the Pentagon effectuated the change in the National Guard's mission from traffic management to riot response.[13]

On January 6, President Donald Trump planned to speak at a rally near the White House.[14] City officials expected thousands of people to attend the rally.[15] Before 9:00am that day, the U.S. Secret Service estimated over 10,000 people were lining up.[16] A Secret Service alert warned of violence: "[S]ome members of the crowd are wearing ballistic helmets, body armor and carrying radio equipment and military grade backpacks . . . ."[17]

President Trump began speaking at noon and urged the rally goers to go to the Capitol and demonstrate "peacefully."[18] At 1:00p.m. the initial wave of protesters began storming the outer police barrier around the Capitol.[19] Minutes later, Vice President Mike Pence gaveled in the Joint Session of Congress to certify the Electoral College vote results.[20]

At 1:49pm U.S. Capitol Police Chief Steven Sund called D.C. National Guard Commanding General William J. Walker to request immediate assistance.[21] Shortly after 2:00pm, protesters broke the first windows of the Capitol and began climbing inside.[22] Suspicious packages, later determined to be pipe bombs, were found outside the Republican National Committee and Democratic National Committee Headquarters between 1:30 and 2:00pm.[23]

Around 2:20pm the Senate and House both recessed and the complex was locked down.[24] Notably, the building was locked down almost an hour and a half after the first barrier was breached and almost a half hour after the first protesters began entering. At around 2:30pm President Trump tweeted "Please support our Capitol Police and Law Enforcement. They are truly on the side of our Country. Stay peaceful!"[25]

Shortly before 3:00pm, rioters broke into the Senate chamber.[26]

EVENTS OF JANUARY 6, 2021

They climbed on the podium, took selfies, and rifled through papers in the room. At 3:36pm White House press secretary Kayleigh McEnany tweeted that President Trump ordered the National Guard to the Capitol.[27] Just before 6:00pm, nearly five hours after the rioting started, police started to secure the Capitol and clear protesters.[28]

The slow response to the violence at the Capitol represents a multi-jurisdictional security breakdown. But the entity that is singularly tasked with protecting the Capitol complex failed to do just that on January 6, 2021.

UNITED STATES CAPITOL POLICE

The U.S. Capitol Police (USCP) was established as part of the Public Buildings Appropriations Act of 1828 "for the care, preservation, orderly keeping, and police, of those portions of the Capitol and its appurtenances, which are in the exclusive use and occupation of either House of Congress, respectively."[29] From an initial force of four officers, USCP has swelled to over 1,800 officers today. The USCP currently has a budget of $602.5 million and received a 20 percent increase in Fiscal Year 2022.[30] USCP oversees a relatively small area of property given its budget, with only a few city blocks of continuous jurisdictional space, stretching from H Street to Potomac Avenue SE and from Third Street SW to Seventh St NE.[31] Unlike most police forces, USCP is also tasked with personal protection for members of Congress in the Capitol and during travel, intelligence gathering for one of the most highly targeted institutions in the world, and operating as a protective force in addition to its policing requirements for members and staff alike. Also, unlike other police forces, USCP is not subject to the Freedom of Information Act.

	USCP	**DC Metropolitan Police**
Budget	FY2022 $602.5 million	FY2021 $578 million
% Increase	20%*	3.3%**
	*from FY2021	**from FY2020

UNITED STATES CAPITOL POLICE

Map of Jurisdiction

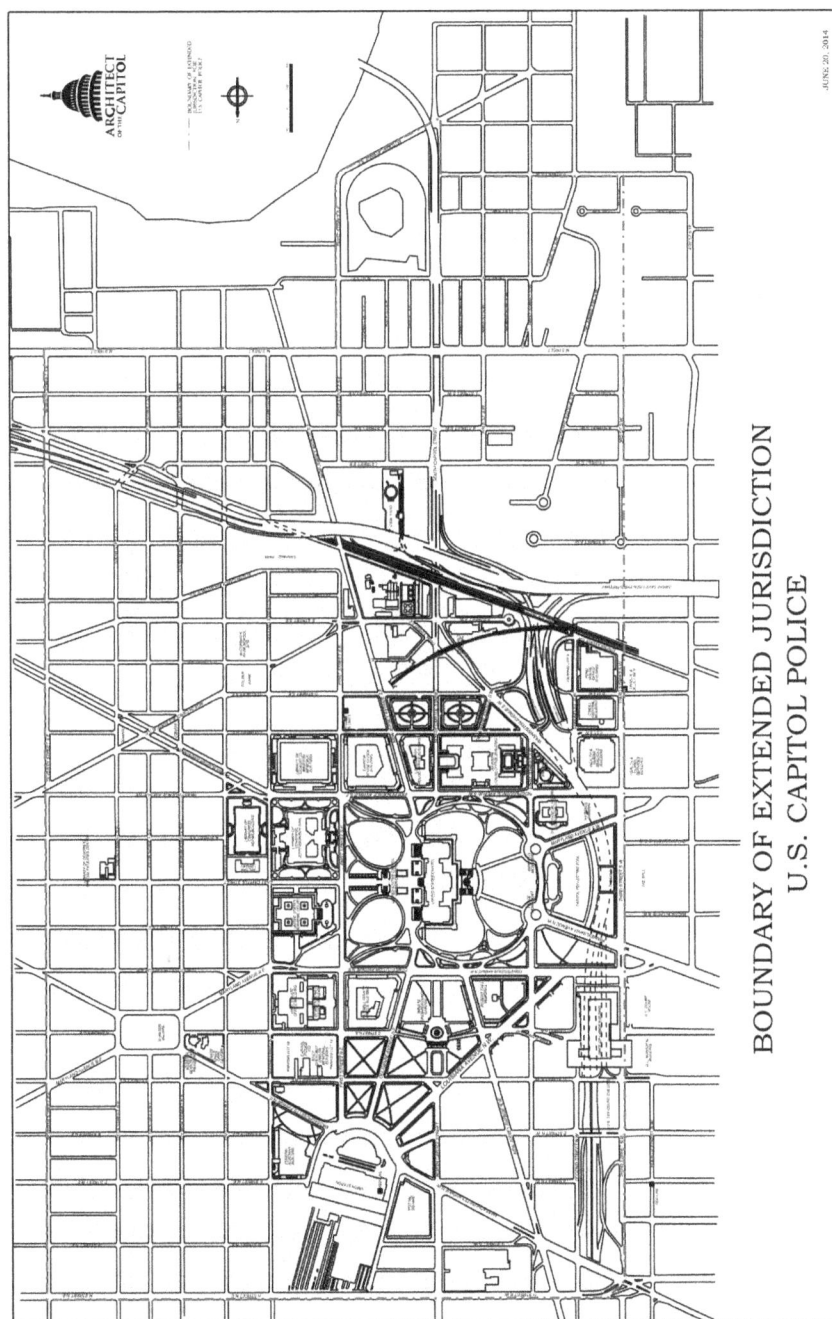

BOUNDARY OF EXTENDED JURISDICTION
U.S. CAPITOL POLICE

UNITED STATES CAPITOL POLICE

A. Background on Recent Violence and Changes to USCP

Over the last three decades, political violence has shaped the USCP and its posture regarding security on the Capitol campus. The bombing in 1995 at the Alfred P. Murrah Federal Building in Oklahoma City led to physical security changes to Federal office buildings across the country, including House and Senate office buildings. The July 24, 1998 shooting of Officer Jacob Chestnut and Detective John Gibson in the U.S. Capitol shocked the Capitol campus.

In particular, the events of September 11, 2001, the 2001 anthrax attack, the 2011 shooting of Rep. Gabrielle Giffords, and the 2017 shooting at the Republican baseball practice, led to major changes to security on and around the U.S. Capitol Complex, including legislative, administrative, and funding changes and a large increase in sworn officers. In 2002, the USCP Chief of Police was given the authority to "deputize members of the DC National Guard and duly sworn law enforcement personnel," and the Senate Sergeant at Arms and USCP chief administrative officer were given the authority to enter into memoranda of understanding with relevant executive branch agencies to respond in case of an emergency.[32] In 2003, the Chief was also given new permissions to increase recruiting incentives to bring in more officers. The same Act allowed:

> [I]n the 'event of an emergency, as determined by the Capitol Police Board or in a concurrent resolution of Congress,' the chief of the Capitol Police is authorized to appoint law enforcement officers from federal, state, and local agencies, and the armed forces (including the National Guard) to serve as Capitol Police officers.'[33]

In 2011, Rep. Gabrielle Giffords and nineteen others were shot by Jared Lee Loughner in a politically-motivated assassination attempt,[34] which led to a review of the USCP security protocols and raised concerns of political violence throughout the country.[35] Concerns about member safety were renewed in 2017 when James Hodgkinson opened fire on Republicans practicing for the annual Congressional Baseball Game, resulting in serious injuries to four people, including Rep. Steve Scalise and a USCP officer.[36]

UNITED STATES CAPITOL POLICE

These incidents of politically motivated violence led to a renewed emphasis on intelligence gathering, better coordination with congressional district offices and more recently, to the creation of regional USCP offices to provide better threat analysis and mitigation in coordination with other law enforcement agencies.

B. USCP Structure

USCP's organizational structure is led by the Chief of Police. Directly under the Chief are the Chief Administrative Officer and two Assistant Chiefs: Assistant Chief of Police for Protective and Intelligence Operations and Assistant Chief of Police for Police and Uniformed Operations. There are five bureaus under the command of the two Assistant Chiefs. Assistant Chief of Police for Protective and Intelligence Operations Yogananda Pittman oversees the Protective Services Bureau (PSB) and the Security Services Bureau (SSB), while Acting Assistant Chief of Police for Police and Uniformed Operations Sean Gallagher oversees the Command and Control, Operational Services, and Uniformed Services Bureaus. The Chief Administrative Officer oversees the Training Services Bureau (TSB). Under those bureaus are 23 Divisions. PSB contains the Dignitary Protection Division (DPD), Investigations Division, and Intelligence and Interagency Coordination Division (IICD).[37]

On January 6, 2021, Steven Sund was Chief of Police. Sund held that position from 2019 until shortly after the attack on January 6, 2021, when Speaker Pelosi asked him to resign.[38] Assistant Chief Pittman replaced Sund and became Acting Chief of Police. J. Thomas Manger became the permanent Chief of Police on July 23, 2021.

On January 6, 2021, Yogananda Pittman was the Assistant Chief of Police for Protective and Intelligence Operations, and Chad Thomas was the Assistant Chief of Police for Police and Uniformed Operations. Thomas stepped down shortly after January 6. Sean Gallagher replaced Chad Thomas as Acting Assistant Chief of Police for Uniformed Operations. Assistant Chief Pittman remains in the position she held on January 6.

UNITED STATES CAPITOL POLICE

Fig. 1: USCP Organizational Structure

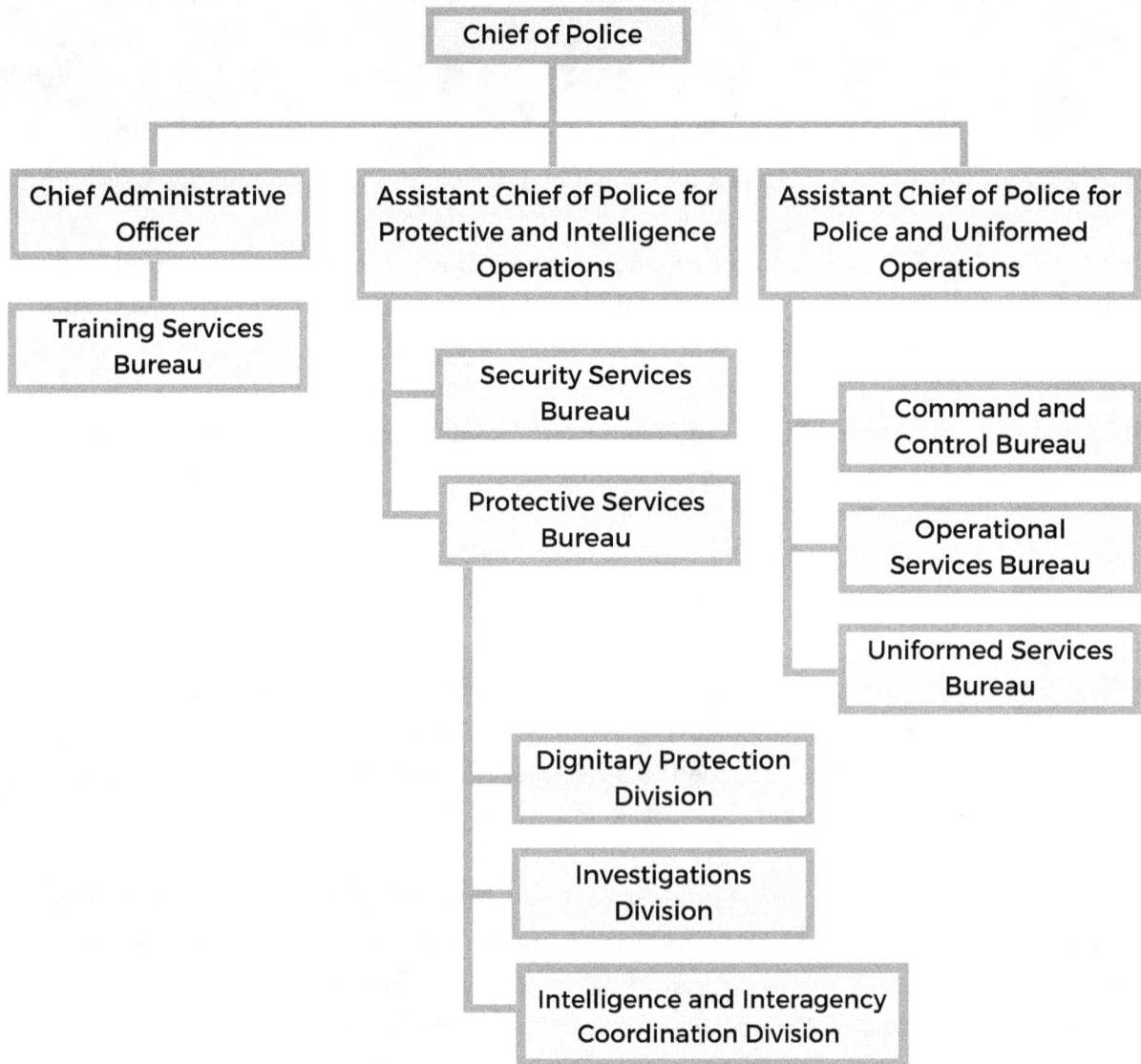

- Chief of Police
  - Chief Administrative Officer
    - Training Services Bureau
  - Assistant Chief of Police for Protective and Intelligence Operations
    - Security Services Bureau
    - Protective Services Bureau
      - Dignitary Protection Division
      - Investigations Division
      - Intelligence and Interagency Coordination Division
  - Assistant Chief of Police for Police and Uniformed Operations
    - Command and Control Bureau
    - Operational Services Bureau
    - Uniformed Services Bureau

CAPITOL POLICE BOARD

The Capitol Police Board (the Board) consists of three voting members—House Sergeant at Arms, Senate Sergeant at Arms, and Architect of the Capitol—and the USCP Chief of Police as an ex officio, non-voting member. Each year, the Chair rotates between the two Sergeants at Arms. The Board is tasked with overseeing the operations of USCP to ensure the safety of the Capitol Complex. But unlike other police oversight bodies, the Board has an extraordinary level of involvement in the operations of USCP, including "designing, installing, and maintaining security systems for the Capitol buildings and grounds," "setting standards for uniforms, furnishing belts and arms," "addressing tort claims," and until recently "designating emergency situations for the purpose of appointing special officers and accepting support services."[39]

The House Committee on Administration and the Senate Committee on Rules and Administration oversee the Board. Following a stator change after the events of January 6, 2021, the two Committees are "authorized to jointly conduct oversight hearings of the Capitol Police Board and may request the attendance of all members of the Capitol Police Board" where all members of the Board shall attend.[40]

The Capitol Police Board originated with the Civil Expenses Appropriations Act of 1867, when responsibility for the Capitol Police was transferred from the Commissioner of Public Buildings to the House and Senate Sergeants at Arms.[41] Initially, the Board only consulted the Architect of the Capitol, but the Architect was later added as a formal voting member and the Board was officially recognized.[42] The structure of the Board remained unchanged for more than one hundred years.

On January 6, 2021, Michael C. Stenger was the Senate Sergeant at Arms and Chair of the Board. He resigned the following day. Mr. Stenger was replaced by Acting Sergeant at Arms Jennifer A. Hemmingway until the current Sergeant at Arms, Karen H. Gibson, was selected.

On January 6, 2021, Paul D. Irving was the House Sergeant at Arms. He also resigned the following day. Mr. Irving was replaced by Acting Sergeant at Arms Timothy P. Blodgett until the current Sergeant at Arms, General William J. Walker, was selected. J. Brett Blanton was the Architect of the Capitol on January 6, 2021 and remains so today.

CAPITOL POLICE BOARD

US Capitol Police Board Structure

Non-Voting Member

> **USCP Chief of Police**

Voting Members

Architect of the Capitol	**Senate Sergeant at Arms**	**House Sergeant at Arms**

The Chair Rotates Between
Sergeants at Arms
Every Year

CAPITOL POLICE BOARD

In response to frustrations related to the opaqueness and bureaucracy of the Board, the House Committee on Appropriations in 2001 required the Government Accountability Office (GAO) to perform an audit. The audit—which was issued in 2003—provided a measure of clarity on the Board's innerworkings and operations. GAO recommended the Board should include the Chief of Police as a non-voting member and adopt a Manual of Procedures, among other things.[43] The report further stated that "The continuing lack of Congressional and other key stakeholder input represents a major gap in the planning efforts' usefulness to USCP, the Congress and others that will need to be addressed as USCP moves forward."[44]

At the time, the USCP indicated a willingness to implement GAO's recommendations and to consult with outside experts to reform the Board's governance structure. In July 2003, then-Capitol Police Chief Terrance Gainer said, "Their criticisms are fair and their suggestions are solid, and we will be working with a vendor to tighten it all up." [45]

The Board was required by the Consolidated Appropriations Resolution of 2003 to examine its mission and to assess the effectiveness and usefulness of its statutory functions.[46] This effort culminated in a 2003 report by the Board to Congress that determined it must align with "corporate governance standards," which broadly included accountability, transparency, and external communication.[47] But, in a harbinger of events to come, the Board failed to implement its own recommendations.

A series of subsequent Government Accountability Office (GAO) reviews of the Board yielded a 2017 omnibus report, "Capitol Police Board: Fully Incorporating Leading Governance Practices Would Help Enhance Accountability, Transparency, and External Communication."[48] Law enforcement experts interviewed for the 2017 report described the Board's responsibilities as "wide ranging" and "atypical."[49] The experts further stated that "typically, law enforcement oversight bodies focus exclusively on a narrow range of issues" that involve long-term strategic planning and budgeting, not interfering with daily operations.[50]

CAPITOL POLICE BOARD

The 2017 report also detailed an array of failures by the Board to implement the recommendations from its 2003 report to Congress.[51] The GAO report recommended "the Board revise its Manual to fully incorporate leading practices, including evaluating its performance, and engage with stakeholders and incorporate their views, as appropriate, on any changes."[52]

The Board rejected several of GAO's key findings and refused to make the recommended changes.[53] In fact, the Board rejected GAO's recommendations with respect to corporate governance as inapplicable because those recommendations were "geared towards private publicly-traded corporations" and defended the Board's structure as "nimble" to allow the USCP to "perform their law enforcement mission with minimal hindrance."[54]

GAO eventually closed its recommendation related to corporate governance as unimplemented and declared the Board non-compliant, only to reinstate the recommendation following the January 6 attack. To date, the GAO recommendation is open.

CAPITOL POLICE BOARD

PHONE (202) 225-2456

UNITED STATES CAPITOL POLICE BOARD
H-124 The Capitol
WASHINGTON, DC 20515

PAUL D. IRVING, Chairman
FRANK J. LARKIN, Member
STEPHEN T. AYERS, FAIA, LEED AP, Member
MATTHEW R. VERDEROSA, Ex-Officio Member

December 14, 2016

Honorable Gene L. Dodaro
Comptroller General
Government Accountability Office
441 G Street, NW
Washington, DC 20548

Dear Mr. Dodaro:

This is in response to the GAO Draft Report, GAO 17-112, "U.S. CAPITOL POLICE BOARD: Fully Incorporating Leading Governance Practices Would Help Enhance Accountability, Transparency, and External Communication". This letter and the attached appendix contain our comments on the Draft Report.

We identified several issues that would benefit from clarification or revision. We highlight some of those issues below and provide additional information concerning all of the issues in the attached appendix.

(1) Capitol Police Board (Board) reporting structure. The Board reports to House and Senate Leadership (Congressional Leadership) vice "committees of jurisdiction", and this fact is missing from the Draft Report's charts. However, it is noted that individual Board members and the Chief of the United States Capitol Police (USCP) meet with various Congressional committees on a regular basis and/or as needed. The current reporting relationship has been validated by Congressional Leadership.

(2) Corporate Governance. The Draft Report relies on the corporate governance model set forth in the "G20/OECD Principles of Corporate Governance" guidelines. However, these guidelines are geared towards private publicly-traded corporations and not Congressional entities such as the USCP or the Board.

(3) Alternative Board structures. The nimble Board structure easily permits the respective chambers to voice any unique and/or specific concerns, through the House or Senate Sergeants at Arms, in a manner that permits the Chief to conduct the day-to-day operational duties and fulfill the responsibilities of the USCP in a manner that comports with sound and established security and law enforcement protocols. The longstanding structure serves legislative branch priorities while maintaining consistent campus-wide security protocols so that the USCP can perform their law enforcement mission with minimal hindrance in protecting the elected officials, staff, and visitors from daily threats.

CAPITOL POLICE BOARD

Recommendations

GAO recommends that the Board revise its Manual to fully incorporate leading practices, including evaluating its performance, and engage with stakeholders and incorporate their views, as appropriate, on any changes. The Board did not state whether it concurred with the recommendation.

Recommendations for Executive Action

Agency Affected	Recommendation	Status
Capitol Police Board	To ensure that the Capitol Police Board's current and any new approaches help enhance accountability, transparency, and effective external communication with its stakeholders, the Board should revise its Manual of Procedures to fully incorporate each of the leading practices for internal control and governance standards discussed in this report. In so doing, the Board should engage stakeholders in the revision process, such as by soliciting their input on any non-statutory changes that could particularly address the concerns stakeholders have raised, and incorporating their views as appropriate. If, in making revisions to its Manual, the Board determines that statutory changes may be helpful to enhance Board operations, then the Board should also engage with stakeholders on such proposed changes.	● Open ⟳ In December 2021 the Board finalized its updates to its Manual and briefed its congressional stakeholders on the changes. We have reviewed the Manual to assess its inclusion of leading practices and conferred with Congressional stakeholders to understand their knowledge of the Manual's updates and the scope and nature of their interactions with the Board. We will continue to monitor the engagement between the Board and its congressional stakeholders as the Board implements its recent updates to the Manual.

B. The Board continues to operate in the dark

The Board similarly failed to address long-standing concerns about a lack of operational transparency and accountability. To date, Board meetings are closed to the public. Beginning in 2022, the Board began sending minutes of their meetings to the oversight committees, but they are months in delay.

The Board does not record how individual members vote on certain measures. More recently, members indicated the Board may begin to record its votes to come into compliance with recommendations in the 2017 GAO Report, but members of the Board were unwilling to commit to doing so during a hearing before the Committee on House Administration in May 2021.[55] Notably, the 2017 GAO report explains that "[t]he six committee stakeholders who felt transparency could be improved said they lacked insight into the Board's decision-making in areas where the committees have responsibilities, such as Capitol Police matters or campus-wide security."[56]

The Board has begun hosting a Capitol Police Board Forum where select members of their oversight entities and Congressional Leadership offices are invited to provide input and feedback to the Capitol Police Board directly.

THE U.S. HOUSE SERGEANT AT ARMS WAS COMPROMISED BY POLITICS AND DID NOT ADEQUATELY PREPARE FOR VIOLENCE AT THE CAPITOL.

On February 9, 2022, Speaker of the House Nancy Pelosi said, "I have no power over the Capitol Police."[57] This is false. Documents provided by the House Sergeant at Arms show how then-House Sergeant at Arms Paul Irving carried out his duties in clear deference to the Speaker, her staff, and other Democratic staff. The Speaker's statement created uncertainty and confusion with respect to the historical reporting structure for the HSAA and USCP.

House Rules dictate in several circumstances that the Sergeant at Arms (SAA) is to report directly to the Speaker of the House, including when the House is in session for, the Sergeant at Arms is to "maintain order under the direction of the Speaker and other presiding officer" and "execute the commands of the House, and all processes issued by authority thereof, directed to the Sergeant at Arms by the Speaker."[58]

Pursuant to the House Rules and for other reasons, the Sergeant at Arms in practice serves under the direction of the Speaker. Accordingly, the Speaker and other Democratic staff routinely have meetings with the Sergeant at Arms and staff. This dynamic is not unique to this Speaker or this House Sergeant at Arms. Indeed, because the Speaker is the highest-ranking Constitutional Officer of the first branch of Government, this structure is neither novel nor controversial. What is novel, however, is a Speaker who denies the relationship and ignores her office's obligation to secure the Capitol, perhaps in an effort to shift blame.

Indeed, Speaker Pelosi exercised her authority with respect to the safety and security of the House of Representatives when she directed the use of magnetometers outside the House chamber in the name of safety.[59] She announced the use of punitive fines for Members who refused to go through the metal detectors.[60] Similarly, she required masks in the House chamber and around the House Office Buildings.

The Speaker also exerted influence on security protocols at the Capitol related to the perimeter fence. Following January 6, 2021, the fence was quickly erected and remained up until July of that year when Congressional leaders started getting pressure to take it down.[61] She also oversaw the fencing that was erected for a purported rally on September 18, 2021, that never materialized, and the State of the Union in March 2022.[62]

THE U.S. HOUSE SERGEANT AT ARMS WAS COMPROMISED BY POLITICS AND DID NOT ADEQUATELY PREPARE FOR VIOLENCE AT THE CAPITOL.

Finally, as the highest-ranking Constitutional Officer, Pelosi used her authority to tap Retired Lieutenant General Russel Honoré to "lead an immediate review of security infrastructure, interagency processes and command and control," following the attack at the Capitol on January 6, 2021.[63]

> **A. The Speaker's office was heavily involved in planning and decision-making before and during the events of January 6, 2021, and micromanaged the Sergeant at Arms.**

Consult Appendix A for a timeline that illustrates how Irving acted in deference to the Speaker and her staff, which was compiled from documents provided by current House Sergeant at Arms William J. Walker. [64]

EARLY DEC 2020	IRVING REMAINED IN CONSTANT COMMUNICATION WITH JAMIE FLEET, A SHARED STAFFER ON SPEAKER PELOSI'S STAFF AND THE STAFF DIRECTOR FOR THE COMMITTEE ON HOUSE ADMINISTRATION, ABOUT PREPARATION FOR THE UPCOMING SWEARING-IN ON JANUARY 3, 2021, THE JOINT SESSION OF CONGRESS ON JANUARY 6, 2021,[65] AND THE INAUGURATION ON JANUARY 20, 2021. IRVING ALSO STAYED IN CONTACT WITH TERRI MCCULLOUGH, SPEAKER PELOSI'S CHIEF OF STAFF ABOUT THE PREPARATIONS.[66]
DEC 8, 2020	IRVING AND HIS STAFF MET WITH DEMOCRATIC STAFF FOR PELOSI, HOUSE ADMINISTRATION AND LEGISLATIVE BRANCH SUBCOMMITTEE OF THE APPROPRIATIONS COMMITTEE WITHOUT REPUBLICAN STAFF PRESENT.
DEC 11, 2020	MCCULLOUGH EMAILED A HOUSE SERGEANT AT ARMS STAFFER TO REQUEST A MEETING. THE EMAIL STATES, "[W]E HAVE HAD A NUMBER OF INTERNAL DISCUSSIONS ABOUT CHOREOGRAPHY AND SAFETY FOR THE OPENING DAY AND ELECTORAL COLLEGE EVENTS. CAN WE GET TOGETHER WITH YOU AND YOUR TEAM EARLY NEXT WEEK TO MAP OUT WHAT WE THINK WE NEED GIVEN THE COMPLEXITIES PRESENTED?"[67] THEY SCHEDULED A MEETING FOR THE FOLLOWING TUESDAY AT 10:00AM.[68]

DEC 15, 2020	MCCULLOUGH AND HOUSE SERGEANT AT ARMS TEAM MET.[69] NO REPUBLICAN STAFF WERE PRESENT OR INVITED.[70]
AFTER MEETING ON DEC 15, 2020	A HOUSE SERGEANT AT ARMS STAFFER SENT IRVING A[71] DRAFT "DEAR COLLEAGUE" LETTER WITH GUIDANCE ON HOUSE ACCESS TO THE CAPITOL FOR OPENING SESSION.[72] IRVING THEN TEXTED JAMIE FLEET FOR CLARIFICATION ON WHO SHOULD REVIEW THE DEAR COLLEAGUE FROM HIS OFFICE.[73] FLEET RESPONDED, SAYING THE INDIVIDUALS FROM THE MEETING EARLIER THAT DAY.[74]

Fig. 5: Text messages between HSAA and Speaker's staff (Dec. 15, 2020)

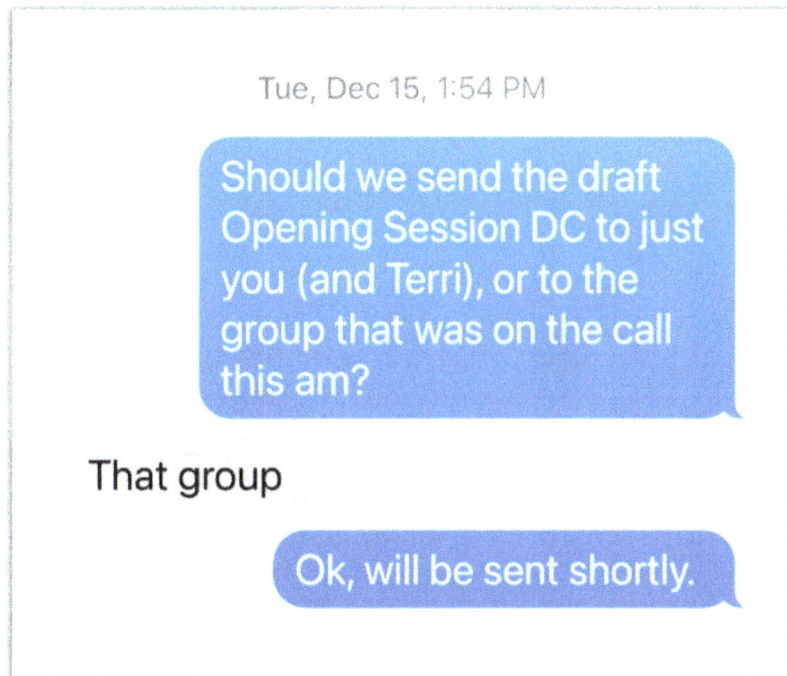

Tue, Dec 15, 1:54 PM

Should we send the draft Opening Session DC to just you (and Terri), or to the group that was on the call this am?

That group

Ok, will be sent shortly.

DEC 21, 2020	IRVING AND HIS STAFF MET WITH DEMOCRATIC STAFF WITHOUT REPUBLICAN STAFF PRESENT.

JAN 3, 2021	●	SERGEANT AT ARMS STAFF CIRCULATED A DRAFT DEAR COLLEAGUE WITH DETAILS FOR JANUARY 6, 2021.[75] IN THE DRAFT, HSAA AND USCP ENCOURAGE MEMBERS AND STAFF TO ARRIVE EARLY, PARK IN GARAGES, AND USE ALTERNATIVE ROUTES TO WALK THROUGH THE PROTEST AREAS.[76] THE LETTER MENTIONS THERE WILL BE ADDITIONAL POLICE ON CAMPUS THAT DAY AND PROVIDES KEY CONTACT INFORMATION. [77]
JAN 4, 2021	●	IRVING AND HIS STAFF MET WITH DEMOCRATIC STAFF WITHOUT REPUBLICAN STAFF PRESENT. [78]
JAN 4, 2021	●	JAMIE FLEET CONTACTED USCP CHIEF STEVEN SUND AND HSAA PAUL IRVING TO SET UP A MEETING WITH THEIR OFFICES AND CHAIRPERSON LOFGREN TO DISCUSS THE SECURITY ARRANGEMENTS FOR JANUARY 6, 2021.[79] THE EMAIL STATES THAT THE "BRIEF SHOULD INCLUDE A DISCUSSION OF USCP STAFFING LEVELS, COORDINATION WITH OTHER DEPARTMENT, AND YOUR DETERMINATION TO EXTEND (OR NOT) THE PERIMETER AROUND THE CAPITOL."[80] IRVING RESPONDED, REQUESTING PERMISSION FOR REPUBLICANS TO JOIN THE BRIEFING.[81] FLEET NEVER RESPONDED OVER TEXT.
JAN 4, 2021	●	IRVING SENT THE DRAFT TO MCCULLOUGH AND FLEET AND REQUESTED "ANY EDITS, COMMENTS, OR CONCERNS."[82] MCCULLOUGH RESPONDED SHORTLY AFTER WITH EDITS. SHE SUGGESTED CLARIFYING PARKING AND EVENT TIMING, AND PROVIDES EDITS TO THE LANGUAGE REGARDING OFFICIAL BUSINESS VISITORS.[83] MCCULLOUGH STATED THAT NOT ALLOWING GUESTS INTO THE CAPITOL (AS THEY PREVIOUSLY DISCUSSED, ACCORDING TO HER) "SENDS A MIXED SIGNAL."[84] LATER IN THE DAY, IRVING TEXTED FLEET, SAYING, "WE'RE MAKING TERRI [MCCULLOUGH]'S EDITS TO THE ELECTORAL COLLEGE AND IF YOU DON'T MIND, I'LL SEND IT TO YOU AND JEN [DAULBY, COMMITTEE ON HOUSE ADMINISTRATION, REPUBLICAN STAFF DIRECTOR] AS A HEADS UP, SO PLEASE ACT SURPRISED."[85] FLEET RESPONDED, "I'M STARTLED!" [86]

Thanks. Davis also wants a briefing; can we do joint or do you prefer separate? Either way obviously works.

Mon, Jan 4, 4:28 PM

We're making Terri's edits to the electoral college DC and if you don't mind, I'll send it to you and Jen as a heads up, so please act surprised.

I'm startled!

JAN 5, 2021	●	MEETING PROCEEDS WITHOUT REPUBLICAN REPRESENTATION.
JAN 5, 2021	●	ANOTHER DRAFT DEAR COLLEAGUE WAS SENT FROM HSAA STAFF TO MCCULLOUGH, FOR MEMBERS AND STAFF REGARDING SECURITY CONCERNS ABOUT THE UPCOMING ELECTORAL COLLEGE COUNT.[87] THE SERGEANT AT ARMS STAFF REQUESTED MCCULLOUGH'S FEEDBACK ON WHAT NEEDED TO BE CHANGED.[88] MCCULLOUGH RESPONDED WITH EDITS.[89]
MORNING OF JAN 6, 2021	●	IRVING AND HIS STAFF MET WITH DEMOCRATIC STAFF WITHOUT REPUBLICAN STAFF PRESENT.

JAN 6, 2021 12:30 PM	●	MCCULLOUGH CALLED IRVING [90]
12:33 PM	●	IRVING CALLED MCCULLOUGH
1:32 PM	●	FLEET MISSED A CALL FROM IRVING
1:33 PM	●	FLEET RETURNED THE CALL FROM IRVING [91]
1:40 PM	●	AFTER CHIEF SUND'S REQUEST FOR ADDITIONAL NATIONAL GUARD ASSISTANCE WAS DELAYED BECAUSE MR. IRVING SAID HE NEEDED TO RUN CHIEF SUND'S REQUEST FOR NATIONAL GUARD TROOPS 'UP THE CHAIN OF COMMAND,'[92] IRVING APPROACHED MCCULLOUGH, AND OTHER STAFF MEMBERS IN THE SPEAKER'S LOBBY BEHIND THE HOUSE CHAMBER. IT WAS THE FIRST TIME MR. IRVING ASKED ABOUT PERMISSION TO SEEK SUPPORT FROM THE NATIONAL GUARD.[93]
1:49 PM	●	MCCULLOUGH SPOKE WITH IRVING TWICE [94]
2:14 PM	●	FLEET CALLED IRVING
2:30 PM	●	MCCULLOUGH CALLED IRVING AGAIN [95]

As demonstrated, the HSAA had a pattern and practice of seeking and obtaining permission from the Speaker for all security decisions. This delayed the request for help from the National Guard. While McCullough passed the note to Speaker Pelosi and received her approval, doing so was not required by the Board – it had become required through years of practice. The Board could have called a meeting and issued an emergency declaration without prior approval from the Speaker. This conclusion is supported by a GAO report issued in February 2022, which states:

> **According to a senior Capitol Police official, the Chief of the Capitol Police was able to ask the Board to determine an emergency, and such a request could be made verbally or in writing. Per the version of section 1974 in place on January 6, 2021, the Board was not required to consult with congressional leadership to do so.**

THE U.S. HOUSE SERGEANT AT ARMS WAS COMPROMISED BY POLITICS AND DID NOT ADEQUATELY PREPARE FOR VIOLENCE AT THE CAPITOL.

Once the Board determined that an emergency exists, the statutory language authorized the Chief of the Capitol Police to appoint officers to serve as special officers of the Capitol Police to provide law enforcement support in the policing of the Capitol complex.[96]

The report issued by Army Lt. Gen Russel Honoré in March 2021 similarly found that the Board's "deliberate decision-making process proved too slow and cumbersome to respond to the crisis in January, delaying requests for critical supplemental resources."[97]

There was also serious concern about optics leading up to and on January 6, 2021. Chief Sund testified that Irving said "optics" were the reason for not sending in the National Guard.[98] Similarly, the Department of Defense (DOD) Inspector General said in a report that "MG [William J.] Walker told us while the DCNG was preparing [for a presentation on DCNG positioning on January 6], Mr. [Ryan C.] McCarthy and senior Army leaders talked about optics, and how DCNG personnel were not to be close to the Capitol."[99]

Later in the report, General James McConville is quoted at length, saying "the general feeling of all those involved [with approving the D.C. RFA] was that the military would have no role, and many people talked about the optics of having military at the Capitol."[100]

Concerns about the optics of military personnel close to the Capitol were shared by Democratic staff in the House of Representatives. On January 5, 2021, a Democratic staffer on the Legislative Branch Subcommittee of the House Appropriations Committee emailed Irving about the placement of National Guard troops. The Democratic staffer said, "I only ask to be ahead of any members who might question a photo or live tv shot that shows National Guard with the Capitol dome in the backdrop."[101]

The March 2022 GAO report states that USCP officers expressed various concerns related to the use of force at the Capitol, including "a concern with optics by leadership"[102] and "several respondents stated that the concern with optics was related to leadership's perception of the desires of Members of Congress."[103]

THE U.S. HOUSE SERGEANT AT ARMS WAS COMPROMISED BY POLITICS AND DID NOT ADEQUATELY PREPARE FOR VIOLENCE AT THE CAPITOL.

The July 30, 2021 USCP OIG report also notes that "Several officers stated that they were deployed without all of their equipment because of 'optics.'"[104] Another officer explained that "at one point in the morning of January 6, they witnessed a USCP Captain ask another officer why they were wearing their helmet and carrying their PR24 baton, ordered the officer to take them off, and said it was 'not the image we want to portray.'"[105] Similarly, another officer told investigators, "there was a debate in [Civil Disturbance Unit] on January 6 about hard gear and 'the officials stated there is going to be media so we don't want you in hard gear.'"[106]

The documents and communications show concerns about the public perception of military personnel at the Capitol and how the use of force by officers against violent protestors were well known among Irving, Democratic leadership, and USCP leadership. Those concerns diminished the capacity of USCP officers to effectively defend the Capitol and prevented the D.C. National Guard from responding to the violence at the Capitol on January 6, 2021.

B. In the lead up to January 6, 2021, the House Sergeant at Arms was distracted, and the Capitol Police Board was dysfunctional.

In addition to preparing for the mounting security threats against the Joint Session on January 6, 2021, Paul Irving and his staff were involved in a number of preparations for other events, including the opening day of the 117th Congress. On December 9, 2020, Irving texted Jamie Fleet about the upcoming Member swearing-in on January 3, 2021: "Just FYI, we have a good plan for the issue you raised regarding opening day."[107] On December 11, 2020, the Assistant House Sergeant at Arms raised concerns with planned renovations to an alternative Chamber space on campus.[108] The Assistant Sergeant at Arms stated:

> [I]f the project were to proceed as scheduled, it would require CAO to make additional equipment purchases and install and configure it for use. This will take several weeks to months after the completion . . . . This leaves the House with no viable on-site alternate chamber option during two highly important event [sic] – Opening Day of the 117th and Joint Session for Electoral Count.[109]

THE U.S. HOUSE SERGEANT AT ARMS WAS COMPROMISED BY POLITICS AND DID NOT ADEQUATELY PREPARE FOR VIOLENCE AT THE CAPITOL.

Later in the day Irving followed up to say that Jamie Fleet weighed in on the situation, agreeing that the work should be postponed.[110] On December 15, 2021, Irving drafted the Opening Session Dear Colleague and requested input from Fleet.[111]

In a text message exchange with a personal friend, Irving said: "when your text came in I was consumed with Opening Day and Electoral College logistics. The week of January 3 will be very challenging.[112]

Irving was simultaneously planning for the Inauguration on January 20, 2021. Typically, the Inauguration is a heavy lift for security staff at the Capitol. It takes up significant resources and requires input from many stakeholders, especially the Chair of the Capitol Police Board, which Irving was prior to January 1, 2021. On December 18, 2020, USCP circulated an invitation to members of the Capitol Police Board to discuss the Inauguration in late January.[113] Notably, Irving met with Chief Sund and law enforcement partners on January 5, 2021, to plan for the Inauguration.[114]

JANUARY 5TH AVIATION THREAT TIMELINE

6:20 PM — IRVING SENT A TEXT TO MICHAEL STENGER, THE SENATE SERGEANT AT ARMS: "ARE YOU MAKING ANY NOTIFICATION REGARDING THE INTEL THAT I'M TOLD IS GOING PUBLIC?"[115] STENGER RESPONDED: "I AM UNDER THE IMPRESSION THAT IT HAS BEEN DEEMED ASPIRATIONAL."[116] IRVING RESPONDED: "AGREE, ALL GOOD."[117] STENGER AND IRVING DID NOT TEXT AGAIN UNTIL JANUARY 11, 2021.[118]

6:50 PM — CBS EVENING NEWS TWEETED: "THE FBI AND FAA ARE LOOKING INTO A BREACH OF AIR TRAFFIC CONTROL FREQUENCIES AFTER A THREAT WAS MADE ABOUT FLYING A PLANE INTO THE CAPITOL TOMORROW."[119] CONGRESSIONAL LEADERSHIP STAFF BEGAN QUESTIONING IRVING AND OTHER MEMBERS OF THE CAPITOL POLICE BOARD ABOUT THE POSSIBLE THREAT.

7:07 PM — A STAFFER FROM SENATE MINORITY LEADER CHUCK SCHUMER'S OFFICE EMAILED CHIEF SUND, COPYING THE HOUSE AND SENATE SERGEANTS AT ARMS AND MAJORITY LEADER MITCH MCCONNELL'S STAFF. THE EMAIL REQUESTED GUIDANCE AS TO HOW TO ADVISE SENATE LEADERSHIP.[120] CHIEF SUND RESPONDED AND SAID USCP WAS INVESTIGATING, ALONG WITH FEDERAL PARTNERS, AND THEY "HAVE NO INFORMATION DEEMING THIS AS CREDIBLE."[121] THEN, WYNDEE PARKER, SPEAKER PELOSI'S NATIONAL SECURITY ADVISOR, REACHED OUT TO IRVING, REQUESTING MORE INFORMATION ON THE AVIATION THREAT.[122] IRVING RESPONDED SHORTLY AFTER TO SAY HE WILL CALL.[123]

8:31 PM — A STAFFER IN SEN. MCCONNELL'S OFFICE RESPONDED TO THE CHAIN OF EMAILS REGARDING THE AVIATION THREAT: "I MUST OBSERVE THERE IS COLLECTIVE CONCERN FROM CONGRESSIONAL LEADERSHIP ABOUT LEARNING ABOUT THIS THREAT REPORTING FROM THE MEDIA RATHER THAN FROM USCP OR HSAA. WE ARE ALSO CONCERNED THAT TIMELY NOTIFICATION MAY NOT HAVE BEEN MADE TO USCP AND HSAA AND ARE MAKING INQUIRIES WITH RESPECTIVE FEDERAL AGENCIES. EVEN IF IT IS NOT A CREDIBLE THREAT, WE WANT TO ENSURE THE SYSTEMS WE HAVE IN PLACE ARE APPROPRIATE." [124]

8:55 PM — DEPUTY CHIEF SEAN GALLAGHER EMAILED HOUSE SERGEANT AT ARMS STAFF, NOTIFYING THEM THAT ONLINE GROUPS FOUND MAPS OF THE CAPITOL TUNNEL SYSTEM, AND THAT THEY WERE PLANNING TO UTILIZE THEM TO CONFRONT MEMBERS OF CONGRESS. FURTHER, THERE WAS AN UPTICK IN MESSAGING OF "GROUPS INTENTIONS OF FORMING A PERIMETER AROUND THE CAMPUS . . . FROM 0600-1000 HOURS IN ORDER TO BLOCK ALL MOC'S FROM GETTING INSIDE OUR PERIMETER TO THE BUILDINGS WITH SPOTS IDENTIFIED FOR DIRECT ACTION." [125]

9:06 PM — THERE IS NO INDICATION THAT GALLAGHER'S WARNING ABOUT THE TUNNELS AND A PERIMETER WERE HEEDED, OR EVEN SHARED WITH USCP OFFICERS, WHO WERE LEFT TO FACE THOUSANDS OF RIOTERS UNPREPARED.

9:06 PM	IN RESPONSE TO THE CHAIN OF EMAILS BETWEEN CHIEF SUND AND SENATE LEADERSHIP STAFF, IRVING SENT AN UNRELATED NOTE TO A SENIOR SAA STAFFER: "THE CHIEF HAS TAKEN [ARCHITECT OF THE CAPITOL] BRETT [BLANTON]'S PLACE. UNBELIEVABLE."[126]
9:09 PM	THE SENIOR SAA STAFFER RESPONDED: "OH GOOD GOD. AND OF COURSE [SEN. MCCONNELL'S STAFFER] HAS NOTHING TO DO RIGHT NOW EXCEPT STIR EVERYONE UP."[127] AT THE SAME TIME, IRVING FORWARDED THE CHAIN OF EMAILS BETWEEN CHIEF SUND AND SENATE LEADERSHIP STAFF TO MICHAEL STENGER WITH A NOTE: "NICE LEADERSHIP ON YOUR SIDE." [128]
9:09 PM	THE SENIOR SAA STAFFER RESPONDED TO IRVING: "EXACTLY THOUGH I THINK [SEN. MCCONNELL'S STAFFER] WOULD STILL GET SPUN UP." [129]
9:13 PM	IRVING EMAILED THE SENIOR SAA STAFFER SEPARATELY. IRVING WROTE: "JUST FYI, I BRIEFED TERRI, JAMIE AND WYNDEE. SO, THEY'RE ALL GOOD. THEY GOT IT BEFORE THE STORY BROKE. STENGER TOLD ME EARLIER HE WASN'T GOING TO TELL ANYONE, AND THIS IS THE RESULT. I LOVE MIKE, BUT SAME STORY, THE [SENATE SERGEANT AT ARMS] DOESN'T GET IT: BRIEF LEADERSHIP IN ADVANCE OF THE STORY"[130] IT IS NOTABLE THAT IRVING ONLY BRIEFED DEMOCRATIC STAFF AND LEADERSHIP.

The communications related to the aviation threat against the Capitol on January 5, 2021, show the ad hoc nature of the Board's response to security events. Even if the various stakeholders had attempted to proceed more deliberately, they would have been stymied by a confusing web of authorities. GAO found the Capitol Police Board had to utilize "various different authorities to obtain assistance from about 2,000 personnel from outside agencies," and they "lacked clear, detailed procedures to guide their decisions about which authority to use or the steps to follow in obtaining assistance." [131] The GAO also found issues with the Board's operations are not limited to January 6, 2021. In their February 2022 report, GAO says that the Department and the Board lack "comprehensive, documented process to assess and mitigate risks," meaning "there is no assurance that the Capitol Police and the Board are not overlooking potential security risks." [132]

USCP FAILED TO ADEQUATELY PREPARE FOR THE EVENTS OF JANUARY 6, 2021

As of November 30, 2022
The USCP Has [133]

1971 Sworn Officers

101 Fewer Than Authorized Cap Of 2072

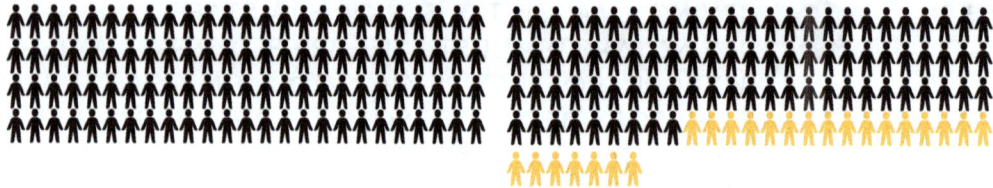

Recommended To Have 2400 Officers

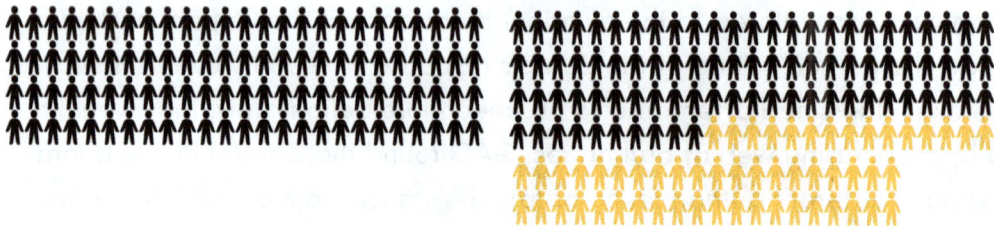

At least 135 Resigned or Retired in the Last Year [134]

USCP FAILED TO ADEQUATELY PREPARE FOR THE EVENTS OF JANUARY 6, 2021

A. USCP lacks adequate equipment

(Stephanie Keith/Reuters)

USCP lacks adequate equipment to protect themselves and the Capitol from an attack like the one on January 6, 2021. This assessment is true today, as it was in various reports by the USCP Office of Inspector General (OIG) and a March 2022 report by GAO. Many officers have outdated equipment, if they have any at all. In fact, according to one USCP source, many veteran officers who gave their equipment to new officers received nothing in return.[135] For example, one Capitol Police officer testified:

USCP FAILED TO ADEQUATELY PREPARE FOR THE EVENTS OF JANUARY 6, 2021

Answer:

[W]hen I first came on the department, they gave us full hard-squad, you know, the "turtle gear" is what we call it. So the plastic gear that you saw. When I got it issued to me, when I came on, 15 years ago, it was probably already 15 years old. Probably about seven years ago they took that equipment away from us to give to newer officers. Including the helmets, gasmasks, and every piece of equipment that went with that.

Question:

What did you get when they gave it to the newer officers?

Answer:

Nothing. Baseball cap. I mean, that's pretty much our equipment now. Which I had on January 6, was nothing, was my baseball cap.[136]

USCP OIG also raised concerns about equipment deficiencies in a series of flash reports. For example, the OIG found the First Responders Unit (FRU)—responsible for the integrity of the perimeter around the Capitol buildings—"did not have the proper resources to complete its mission."[137] More specifically, the FRU was "not equipped with adequate less lethal weapons such as Pepper-Ball and Stinger-Ball weapon systems."[138] The USCP OIG found this equipment would have been helpful, "because of [its] ability to incapacitate a person or a group of people without directly escalating to lethal means" and "would be effective assisting officers when confronting violent crowds similar to the ones encountered during the events of January 6, 2021."[139]

Further, according to the OIG, what equipment the officers did have on January 6, 2021 was ineffective or compromised. According to the OIG's second flash report, "officers witnessed riot shields shattering upon impact," and crucial less-lethal weapons and munitions were not deployed because they were expired.[140] In some cases, equipment was disregarded because USCP officers were not trained to use it.[141]

The lack of effective training is a longstanding, USCP-wide issue that contributed to confusion and dysfunction on January 6, 2021. The Office of Inspector General issued a series of flash reports—report nos. 2, 3, 4, 5, 6, and 7—that all describe specific concerns

USCP FAILED TO ADEQUATELY PREPARE FOR THE EVENTS OF JANUARY 6, 2021

B.   Systemic Department-Wide Training Failures

about the lack of training and certification throughout the USCP.

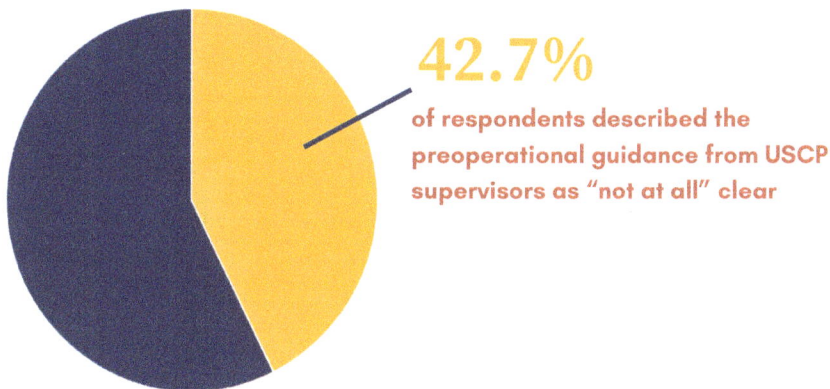

42.7%

of respondents described the preoperational guidance from USCP supervisors as "not at all" clear

Over Half Respondents Expressed That[142]

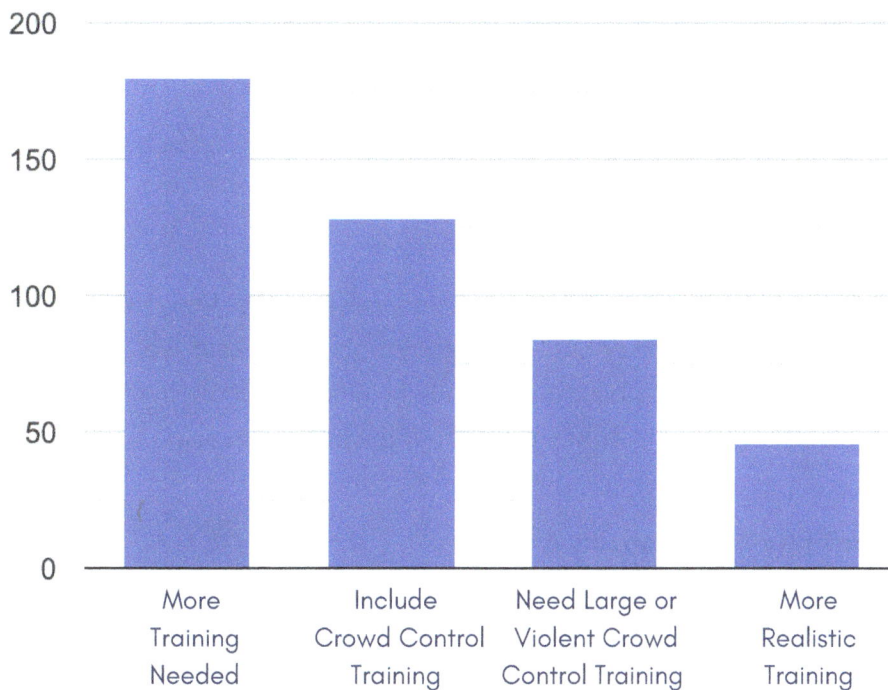

USCP FAILED TO ADEQUATELY PREPARE FOR THE EVENTS OF JANUARY 6, 2021

These deficiencies are attributable in part to a high "officer utilization rate" and short staffing, but also because USCP has a decentralized training structure that lacks accountability to ensure training is completed.[143] Because individual units are responsible for their own training, USCP is largely unable to track who is trained and when, and commanding officers are never held to account if training is not completed.[144] According to information obtained by investigators, this issue has only gotten worse since January 6, 2021 because of dwindling resources.

More specifically, officers are not being trained on how to use what little equipment is issued to them, and officers who move into leadership positions are not sufficiently trained to develop management skills.[145] A USCP officer told investigators that training now occurs online, which is insufficient to prepare a police officer for real-world scenarios. USCP Chief Manger explained that the current shortage of officers limits the availability of officers to be pulled from assignments to receive training.[146] One USCP officer testified:

> **Answer:**
> [T]he baton I carried on January 6th, for instance, I got trained on in the academy. I haven't been trained on it since. So, obviously we do firearms twice a year, but that's about it for training on our equipment.
>
> **Question:**
> What's your expectation of training with your baton?
>
> **Answer:**
> Baton should be, at minimum, once a year, to every other year. I mean, it's a piece of equipment where we could actually hurt or kill somebody with, and we're never trained on it. We asked multiple times to be trained on it, we just were always told, never had the manpower or we just carry it. That's pretty much what we're told.
>
> **Question:**
> And you were carrying that on January 6th?
>
> **Answer:**
> I not only carried it, I used it on January 6th, yes.

USCP FAILED TO ADEQUATELY PREPARE FOR THE EVENTS OF JANUARY 6, 2021

> **Question:**
>
> Without any training from Capitol Police?
>
> **Answer:**
>
> Not in 15 years, no.[147]

Uniformed officers also raised concerns about the fact that certain segments of USCP leadership do not have experience in the jobs they command. A USCP source stated:

> **Answer:**
>
> So we have different bureaus in our department. We have [Uniformed Services Bureau], which I am. We're the uniform guys. And then we have the [Protective Services Bureau], which is the Protection. So, if you look at our regime right now, we have no upper management in the Deputy Chief position or up that has been a commander of USB. Not one. So, when it comes to our positions, which are roughly 1,200 to 1,300 officers –
>
> **Question:**
>
> Out of how many?
>
> **Answer:**
>
> I think we have 1,800 right now. Or less. I don't even know what the numbers are now. **But, we have someone in position who doesn't know our job, because they've never commanded our job.**[148]

A shortage of officers, a lack of training, and insufficient equipment does not entirely explain the failures at the Capitol on January 6, 2021. But the documents and testimony make clear that more officers who were better equipped and trained could have effected a starkly different outcome.

Likewise, had USCP leadership and middle-management been adequately trained, USCP would have been better prepared and more capable of responding to the crisis. These vulnerabilities were well known—the USCP OIG and GAO identified these very concerns, repeatedly. Such longstanding and pervasive department-wide problems are consequences of the Capitol Police Board's tendency to ignore recommendations from the OIG and GAO prior to January 6, 2021, among other things.

USCP INTELLIGENCE FAILURES ARE DIRECTLY TO BLAME FOR THE LACK OF PREPAREDNESS ON JANUARY 6, 2021.

The failure to limit the scope of the attack on January 6, 2021, was as much a management failure as an intelligence failure. New leadership of the intelligence division restructured the open-source intelligence team, moving the group into a reactionary posture, and actively opposed a more proactive approach to preventing violence and disruptions at the Capitol. The redesigned intelligence division was fragmented, and Capitol Police leadership were not fully informed about the severity of the threats against the Joint Session of Congress on January 6, 2021.

USCP houses two intelligence-related divisions, the Intelligence and Interagency Coordination Division (IICD) and the investigations division.[149] The investigations division is bifurcated into two sections: the threat assessment section (TAS) and the intelligence operations section (IOS).[150] All the intelligence operations of USCP reside in the Protective Services Bureau, which is overseen by the Assistant Chief of Police for Protective and Intelligence Operations.[151]

USCP historically is not a "collector" but rather a "consumer" of intelligence.[152] But in recent years, USCP has attempted with mixed results to transition toward intelligence collection.

Norm Grahe led IICD for many years. Under his leadership in January of 2013, IICD stood up an open-source section tasked with gathering open-source intelligence about the goals and plans of groups who seek to harm Members of Congress and disrupt congressional activities or large events like high-profile confirmation hearings or the Joint Session of Congress to certify election results.[153] The open-source section proved largely effective at preventing harm to Members of Congress, staff, or events at the Capitol until its restructuring in the months leading to January 6, 2021.

IICD regularly produces intelligence products for USCP and the House and Senate Sergeants at Arms, including a Daily Intelligence Report, Special Event Assessments, and Congressional Event Assessments.[154]

USCP INTELLIGENCE FAILURES ARE DIRECTLY TO BLAME FOR THE LACK OF PREPAREDNESS ON JANUARY 6, 2021.

Daily Intelligence Reports are sent to security leaders in the Capitol with information and analysis of relevant developments on and around the Capitol campus. Special Events Assessments focus on upcoming, high-profile events on and around the Capitol campus.[155] USCP Leadership, the House and Senate Sergeants at Arms, and House and Senate leadership routinely consult IICD regarding upcoming events, threat alerts to the Capitol, and the threat environment more broadly. They also coordinate with relevant staff in USCP to make their intelligence operational, and they are responsible for ensuring intelligence is distributed up the chain of command.[156] For IICD, this means passing information to the Assistant Chief of Police for Protective and Intelligence Operations, the House and Senate Sergeants at Arms, and DPD.

But as the second USCP OIG flash report on the events of January 6, 2021 notes, intelligence is decentralized within the USCP. This fragmentation creates inefficiencies with respect to the distribution and consumption of intelligence products.[157] Further, the report notes that distributing intelligence throughout the entire department was challenging before and during the events of January 6, and that guidance for IICD was "very ambiguous."[158]

The USCP OIG's fifth flash report described the subsequent effect on preparation down the chain of command. In interviews conducted by the OIG, "one officer stated at one point in the morning of January 6, they witnessed a USCP Captain ask another officer why they were wearing their helmet and carrying their PR24 baton, ordered the officer to take them off, and said it was 'not the image we want to portray.'"[159]

USCP INTELLIGENCE FAILURES ARE DIRECTLY TO BLAME FOR THE LACK OF PREPAREDNESS ON JANUARY 6, 2021.

Fig. 4: Excerpt from January 6, 2021 Daily Intelligence Report

1/6/2021- Hours- TBD	Million MAGA March/US Capitol (Possibly)	Event Details: On December 19, 2020, MPD discovered a tweet from the Million MAGA March twitter account indicating the group would be planning their biggest protest ever in support of President Trump. NFI is available as to the time. Approximate attendance: TBD-Twitter feed has 3000 retweets and 4900 likes. Source: https://twitter.com/milionmagamarch/status/1340217633715720194?s=21 and https://www.thegatewaypundit.com/2020/12/president-donald-trump-calls-protest-dc-jan-6-says-will-wild/	Improbable- **PRO-TRUMP group-** The 6th is the day Congress meets for a Joint session to confirm the electoral vote, thus making it possible the Million Magi March folks could organize a demonstration on USCP grounds. Women for America First has permitted on USCP grounds and Freedom Plaza parade permit through MPD and has been the permitted portion of previous Million MAGA Marches. There is also growing talk of opposing the Million MAGA March folks by counter demonstrators with no clear plans by those groups at this time.

Source: *Daily Intelligence Report* for January 6, 2021.

A. There had not been an intelligence failure at this scale in the USCP Intelligence Division prior to the Joint Session of Congress on January 6, 2021.

During preparation for large events, IICD is typically tasked with collecting open-source intelligence about groups who may intend on causing a disruption, analyzing it, and passing it to USCP leadership so it can be operationalized.[160]

USCP INTELLIGENCE FAILURES ARE DIRECTLY TO BLAME FOR THE LACK OF PREPAREDNESS ON JANUARY 6, 2021.

For example, during the confirmation hearings of U.S. Supreme Court Justice Brett Kavanaugh, IICD relied on the expertise of their analysts and began scouring open-source social media posts of groups that are notorious for causing problems with such event.[161] After gathering relevant intelligence, the IICD team typically designated a team lead to write an intelligence assessment that would be disseminated to Capitol Police leadership.[162] The preparation in the lead up to the Kavanaugh hearings was illustrative. For example, one analyst described the process of gathering and disseminating the information for the Kavanaugh hearings:

> **We also worked on the special [event]/special permit assessments. They would come from Special Events to us and we would contact the organizer, the spokesperson and get some background information. We would look do they have a history of protesting or causing disruptions on Capitol Hill? And we would write all that up in an assessment and then send that up through our chain of command.** [163]
>
> * * *
>
> **[I]f we had stuff coming up during the week, we would send it out, either in email, or in assessment -- I believe we wrote an assessment . . . saying that we expected large crowds and disruptions to the confirmation hearings and, that we had a number of protests that were planned, some that were permitted. That they went through Special Events and found a permit for certain areas.** [164]

Preparation for such an event was a team effort that relied heavily on the expertise of the analysts.[165] One analyst testified about how the information moved up and down the chain of command within IICD under then-IICD Director Norm Grahe:

> **Answer:**
> [Analyst] would gather up, receive all the information. [They] would write up a draft of the intelligence assessment.

USCP INTELLIGENCE FAILURES ARE DIRECTLY TO BLAME FOR THE LACK OF PREPAREDNESS ON JANUARY 6, 2021.

Answer:
And then [they] would provide that to Mr. Grahe for review, and then there is a daily process. Mr. Grahe would say what they want. [They] would send him a draft. He would say, make these changes. It would come back down. So it's a circle. We collect information. It goes up the chains. It gets evaluated –

Question:
Constantly getting updated.

Answer:
Updated. There's more questions. They say, okay. I see this information. It raises this question. And then it would be sent back down to us. And . . . they had daily meetings referencing, creating this intelligence assessment. [166]

IICD Director Norm Grahe held weekly intelligence briefings for Capitol Police leadership to include an "inspector and above meeting, and a meeting with captains and then . . . a meeting with both House and Senate Sergeant at Arms . . . to discuss . . . upcoming demonstrations and things of concern." [167]

One IICD analyst testified:

Answer:
[The intelligence briefing] was every Tuesday, we had a weekly standing meeting in the SCIF conference room. At 10 o'clock we briefed inspectors and above. At 11 o'clock it was captains. And then at 12 o'clock it was the House and Senate Sergeant at Arms . . . . [168]

* * *

So, we would get those people coming over and we would brief them. And it was a, death by Power Point. And I would go through, "Okay, these are the permitted events coming up for this week."

USCP INTELLIGENCE FAILURES ARE DIRECTLY TO BLAME FOR THE LACK OF PREPAREDNESS ON JANUARY 6, 2021.

Answer:

And then we would have them rated, whether it was going to be something of concern, if [it] was a remote possibility, or yeah, we were concerned about this. . . [W]e had the size, how many people were coming, what areas they were going to be in, what their mission statement was. So that way they understood.

Question:

In the lead up to Kavanagh, was it once a week, or did you have increased briefings?

Answer:

As we got more information, we would start sending it out ahead of time . . . .[169]

* * *

I would think that there was an occasional email maybe the night before, saying, "Okay, we got information, this group's going to assemble at this place." [170]

* * *

[Norm Grahe] had his distribution list that he would send it out to. But, if he had any questions or he wanted something clarified, he would send it back for a correction, which very rarely did I get anything back for a correction. And he would send it out to basically lieutenants and above, whoever needed that information.

Question:

And the assessments, like you said, were also rolling, they would come out when you had new information?

Answer:

 Yes. And I actually used to say, "Update number one . . ." and then put it on top of the previous of assessment. [171]

* * *

Question:

So, in the lead up to the Kavanagh hearings, how often, let's say like the week of the hearings, how often are you sending out these assessments?

USCP INTELLIGENCE FAILURES ARE DIRECTLY TO BLAME FOR THE LACK OF PREPAREDNESS ON JANUARY 6, 2021.

Answer:

The assessment was probably sent out maybe once that week. But then we were on the phone verbally and we were, because I had various members, they would call me, the department members, . . . they would all be calling me, to say, "Do you have any more information." And I would say, "Yeah, I was just getting ready to send this out to you guys." And CDU, they would always call, whoever was commanding CDU would call me. [172]

* * *

Question:

And how would you grade the success of your, you know, your team, and what it was able to do at, with the Kavanagh hearings?

Answer:

I think we were very successful, because the hearings were able to go on, we made almost 800 arrests that week. We were well aware of who was going to be where, what was going on, what was going to be expected, what the groups were planning. And so, our officers knew that. [173]

Grahe relied on his analysts—who are intelligence experts—to prepare the intelligence for the assessments. Grahe then sent out the assessments to USCP leaders and officers to help inform their decisions regarding how best to keep the Capitol safe. For example, one analyst testified:

Answer:

[I]f I would have had a concern, which has happened numerous times, I would say, I would go to him and say, "This demonstration's coming up and I'm having a bad feeling about it."

Question:

Right.

USCP INTELLIGENCE FAILURES ARE DIRECTLY TO BLAME FOR THE LACK OF PREPAREDNESS ON JANUARY 6, 2021.

Answer:
And he'd say, "Get me facts and I'll go upstairs."

Question:
Okay.

Answer:
And I would give him the facts, give them to him, and he would go up to the 7th floor and tell them, . . . we would sit in briefings and he would take me into some of the briefings, you know, and I could tell them, "I'm feeling bad about this because X,Y, and Z."

Question:
Right. So when he went to the 7th floor, who was he telling?

Answer:
He was telling the assistant chiefs and the Chief. The upper management.[174]

IICD prepared by constantly socializing the intelligence. Grahe and his team knew the more information USCP leadership had, the better they could prepare. That mentality also applied from the top down. The more information the analysts had, the more effective they could be at creating an intelligence assessment. A USCP source testified:

Answer:
And [they] would come back into the office. We would all sit in a circle, and [analyst team lead] would say this is what came up during my meeting with Mr. Grahe. And then [analyst team lead] would send out assignments.

Question:
So [they] would make sure everyone was informed on the updates, make sure that whatever was needed was assigned out, and everyone was on the same page?

USCP INTELLIGENCE FAILURES ARE DIRECTLY TO BLAME FOR THE LACK OF PREPAREDNESS ON JANUARY 6, 2021.

Question:

At what point is that then socialized with Capitol Police leadership or whoever needs to know up the chain? Is it happening the whole time?

Answer:

Yes. [175]

The analysts sought out and maintained relationships with outside agencies such as the Federal Bureau of Investigation, the Department of Homeland Security, U.S. Park Police, Washington D.C. Metro Police Department, and Secret Service. [176] The IICD analysts kept an open line of communication with those agencies to share important information. [177] A USCP source stated:

Between Mr. Grahe and commanders on the operational side, they were having daily side conversations through their personal connections. And so was [USCP analyst]. [USCP analyst] was with other agencies. [USCP analyst] has great relationships with Park Police, MPD, Secret Service Police. So daily conversations with all of these people. And then . . . everybody is in the know with the latest information. [178]

Norm Grahe intended to retire after the November 2020 election and Jack Donohue and Julie Farnam were hired to replace him as the Director and Assistant Director respectively. Farnam joined just before the election and Donohue joined weeks later. [180] In the lead up to January 6, 2021, Donohue and Farnam reported to Deputy Chief Kim Schneider, who was replaced by Sean Gallagher. [181] Sean Gallagher reported to Assistant Chief of Police for Protective and Intelligence Operations Yogananda Pittman who reported to Chief Sund. [182]

Farnam's only previous intelligence experience was in the Immigration Vetting Division of U.S. Citizenship and Immigration Services. [183] Because Farnam had no relevant intelligence experience, Grahe intended to remain on the job to train her. [184] According to a USCP source who testified to investigators, Farham declined. [185] In her new role as the assistant director of IICD, she attempted to remake the USCP. [186]

USCP INTELLIGENCE FAILURES ARE DIRECTLY TO BLAME FOR THE LACK OF PREPAREDNESS ON JANUARY 6, 2021.

B. Changes to the Intelligence Division after November 2020 caused the intelligence failures on January 6, 2021.

Prior to November 2020 when USCP prepared for a special event, the intelligence analysts in the open-source section worked together to gather intelligence and create an assessment for each event. The USCP Special Events section sends all permits to IICD. [187] One analyst would typically be tapped to serve as de facto team lead. [188] That analyst would assign work out to the team and had visibility into what each team member was working on. [188] The team lead tracked and gathered all the information from the analysts and then prepared an intelligence assessment to send to the Special Events section to inform decisions about granting or denying the permit, and where to assign the group on the Capitol grounds. [190]

After November 2020—when Farnam took over for Norm Grahe—that process changed. [191] The USCP OIG found that those changes left USCP worse off. According to the OIG, as of January 6, 2021, "IICD [lacked] comprehensive policies and procedures relevant to their open source intelligence gathering efforts," and "IICD did not always include previous reporting into later assessments." [192]

USCP INTELLIGENCE FAILURES ARE DIRECTLY TO BLAME FOR THE LACK OF PREPAREDNESS ON JANUARY 6, 2021.

FARNAM WAS ONLY ON THE JOB FOR APPROXIMATELY **10 WEEKS** BEFORE THE ATTACK

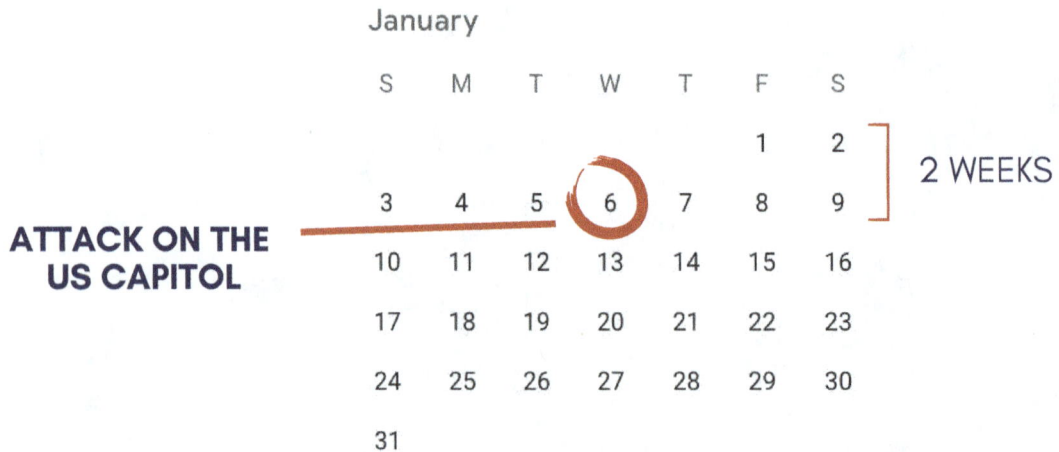

November

S	M	T	W	T	F	S
1	2	3	4	5	6	7
8	9	10	11	12	13	14
15	16	17	18	19	20	21
22	23	24	25	26	27	28
29	30					

NOVEMBER 2020 ELECTION → 3

NORM GRAHE RETIREMENT DATE

4 WEEKS

December

S	M	T	W	T	F	S
		1	2	3	4	5
6	7	8	9	10	11	12
13	14	15	16	17	18	19
20	21	22	23	24	25	26
27	28	29	30	31		

4 WEEKS

January

S	M	T	W	T	F	S
					1	2
3	4	5	6	7	8	9
10	11	12	13	14	15	16
17	18	19	20	21	22	23
24	25	26	27	28	29	30
31						

2 WEEKS

ATTACK ON THE US CAPITOL → 6

51

USCP INTELLIGENCE FAILURES ARE DIRECTLY TO BLAME FOR THE LACK OF PREPAREDNESS ON JANUARY 6, 2021.

In a May 2022, review, the USCP Inspector General found that "up until December/January 2020/2021, or possibly a little earlier, IICD was divided into an unofficial 'Open Source Section (OSS)' and 'Intelligence Analysis Section (IAS),'" and that "IICD officials changed the process around that time, eliminated OSS, and made all [Intelligence Research Specialists] responsible for performing open source searches."[193]

Even though there had not been an intelligence-based security failure prior to Farnam's arrival, she believed the analyst team was not sufficiently performing its job.[194] Upon her arrival, Farnam immediately began disassembling the open-source section.[195] She described the team as "struggling with some of [the] taskings" she assigned.[196] She testified, "I felt coming on board I had to do a lot of the analytic work myself. I'm not going to speak for Jack [Donahue], but I know the two of us did a lot of, like, the analyst type work in the beginning because the team didn't have the capability."[197]

The analyst team lead, however, described Farham as non-responsive and hostile to the analyst's effort to provide support. The analyst testified:

Answer:

[T]he special event permits would come to me, from Special Events and I would assign them out. I'd log them in and assign them out. So that way I could always tell where they were and I could go put my hands on them at any given time. . . . I would assign out a special event permit, and a half an hour later she would assign it to somebody else.

So, I would send [Julie Farnam] an email and say, "You don't have to worry about this, I take care of this, and we'll get it done." She never responded. In the [first] phone call [with Farnam] I was told I was insubordinate because I was explaining the process to her and no underling should ever tell a supervisory what to do.[198]

* * *

And then I got written up over the weekend for that, because I was unprofessional and unwelcoming. So I got a 550 the following Monday morning.

USCP INTELLIGENCE FAILURES ARE DIRECTLY TO BLAME FOR THE LACK OF PREPAREDNESS ON JANUARY 6, 2021.

Question:
[Y]ou were written up because you were unwelcoming?

Answer:
Yes. And unprofessional.[199]

Analysts and other USCP sources interviewed by the Committee described how the changes implemented by Farnam undermined their work. Analysts testified to investigators that the section became "nonfunctional" immediately upon Farnam's arrival.[200] One analyst testified that Farnam's changes—which were not formally communicated—stripped experts out of the roles in which their experience could be leveraged.

The analyst testified:

> [S]he basically didn't come out and say, "I'm shutting out the open-source Section," but she started assigning our taskings to other analysts upstairs, who were unfamiliar with what we did.[201]
>
> * * *
>
> [W]e have very specific lanes that we worked in, for a reason. I mean, because there's so much one person can't possibly keep up with everything. And we developed expertise in those areas. My expertise was with the groups that used to come up to the Hill to demonstrate all the time. I checked with their social media pages every day. I knew who the key players were. And I could tell, from experience, this is going to be a problem, or this isn't going to be a problem.[202]

Similarly, another analyst testified, "That unit was disbanded by her almost on day one. We, at the time of January 6, we were not doing proactive searches of social media like we had been before. We were strictly reactive and responding to requests for information."[203]

USCP INTELLIGENCE FAILURES ARE DIRECTLY TO BLAME FOR THE LACK OF PREPAREDNESS ON JANUARY 6, 2021.

The analyst further stated that Farnam removed the open-source experts from the process to consolidate power for herself to the detriment of the safety and security of the Capitol.[204] One analyst stated:

> **[W]hen we identified a threat, we would assess the threat and create a notification sheet and send it to the threat assessment section. But we would copy everybody in the division, so everybody had eyes on threats that were being made. And she changed that policy to say it would only be her and the director copied on the email sent to threats, not all of the analysts. So when in the lead-up to January 6, many people, many of the analysts weren't even aware of the vitriol of threats that were coming through on social media.[205]**

Those changes had consequences. Due to the sudden changes to the structure of the open-source section, experienced analysts missed clear signs of violence and important information that indicated a threat to the Capitol. One analyst testified:

> **Answer:**
> [T]he standard procedure up to that is there would be an analyst assigned as the lead for that event, and that analyst would track the event from notification to the final assessment. And that analyst would receive all the information from the other analysts as the point person, and produce a draft assessment. And that draft assessment would go to the director. And as we mentioned before, it's a cyclical process, going on from the time you know about it, until the final assessment. Whereas in this case, Ms. Farnham said herself was going to be the point person for the assessment. So all the information was sent to her. There was no analyst assigned to follow or track the event.
>
> **Question:**
> [W]hat does it tell you as an expert if the same person is getting a permit for every spot around the Capitol? Would that raise a flag to you?

USCP INTELLIGENCE FAILURES ARE DIRECTLY TO BLAME FOR THE LACK OF PREPAREDNESS ON JANUARY 6, 2021.

Answer:
Absolutely.[206]

* * *

I would point out that one of our duties in the intelligence unit is to conduct an event assessment that is predicated on the assessment permit. So special events section gets a permit. And while they are doing their job, they notify us, and we conduct an event assessment as well. And our final assessment goes back to special events section. And that would be all coordinated. Prior to that, it would come through [the analysts' team lead]. So, if -- but in this case, it was being coordinated and everything was going through Ms. Farnham. So we had . . . no idea what permits were being applied for.[207]

According to the analysts, Farnam regularly assigned tasks, reassigned tasks, and then locked the completed assessment files so the analysts could not access them, even as those analysts were working on the same issue.[208] A USCP source told investigators:

[S]he kept re-assigning things to people, different people, because that was her version of "cross-training" everybody, which she basically came in and said okay everybody up and change chairs immediately. And we became non-functional, because nobody knew what they were doing, and we had to learn the job. And we were trying to learn from the people that did it before, and it was just a lot of confusion and things were being written up in wrong formats. . . . Files were moved around. Files were re-named. There's a locked file.[209]

If Farnam received an assessment and was not satisfied with the final product, she rewrote it.[210] Analysts never saw the final intelligence product. In some cases, Farnam locked the file and analysts could not access it.[211] The final product was shared outside the division, but analysts still did not have access to the final version.[212]

One analyst stated:

USCP INTELLIGENCE FAILURES ARE DIRECTLY TO BLAME FOR THE LACK OF PREPAREDNESS ON JANUARY 6, 2021.

The way we functioned before was, each section had our own case log, and we would put everything on there and draw the next case number. And we could easily go back and find—and it would be saved under the file name, you know, "21-O- --" we could easily go put our hands on that document. Now, we can't put our hands on documents if we have to go back and research something. Files are constantly being moved around. Folder names are being changed all the time. So you're always hunting for things.[213]

The documents and testimony show that immediately upon joining the USCP, and without time to acclimate, Farnam began to dismantle the systems that had kept the Capitol safe for so long.

In fact, upon her arrival at IICD, Farnam reassigned analysts to projects outside the scope of their regular work and required analysts to perform jobs they had not been trained to do. One analyst described the breakdown of productivity.

The analyst testified:

Answer:

I mean, the one analyst, [USCP analyst], was told to monitor a protest and [they] had never done that before. So, [they] didn't have a clue how to start to do that. And [they] didn't have the accounts, the social media accounts established, to be able to monitor on social media. I mean, how functional is that? And I was getting assigned threats and things like that that I hadn't worked on, it took me a while to knock the dust off to do that because I'd been so focused on demonstrations.

USCP INTELLIGENCE FAILURES ARE DIRECTLY TO BLAME FOR THE LACK OF PREPAREDNESS ON JANUARY 6, 2021.

Answer:

But I was one of the fortunate ones that I have kind of worked all those jobs in IICD, but some of those analysts hadn't; they'd always been pigeon-holed. And they were being plucked out and stuffed into another chair. And it took a while to get our feet on the ground. And even now, I would say nobody's 100 percent comfortable with their job. Because it's constant, it's a constantly changing environment. She's changing forms. She's changing names of things. She's changing logs. It's just a constant flux. You can't ever get your feet on the ground, if that makes sense?[214]

Question:

And these changes began when she arrived in November?

Answer:

Yes.

Question:

Do you feel that the team had their feet on the ground by December, when the threats were escalating as it relates to January, or –

Answer:

No, definitely not.[215]

* * *

Because we were still being shifted around and assigned different projects and by December some of the analysts were being assigned ridiculous projects. There [were] three analysts at least that were working on an assassination project for her. They were told to research all political assassinations in the history of the world, worldwide. And I'm, when they told me that's what they were assigned, I was like, "But that's like a Ph.D. dissertation, that's not an assessment document, or an intelligence document." I said, and what is that, somebody being assassinated in 1700 in England, what does that have to do with us now? I could see if it was focused more on the U.S. political assassination attempts and things like that. But it was everything.

USCP INTELLIGENCE FAILURES ARE DIRECTLY TO BLAME FOR THE LACK OF PREPAREDNESS ON JANUARY 6, 2021.

Question:

And when was that assigned?

Answer:

That was in December.

Question:

And how many analysts were working on it?

Answer:

Three. We had two analyst --

Question:

How many analysts are there total?

Answer:

I think there's like eleven or twelve of us at that time. And one of them, it was two analysts and a light-duty officer who was functioning as an analyst. And they got 43 pages written, sent it to her for approval, and they've never heard anything else on that project.[216]

Farnham discussed these "research projects." She testified:

[O]ne of the projects was to look at assassinations and assassination attempts against elected officials because we have seen a huge surge in threats. . . . So, that information is helpful to see, you know, are there patterns . . . . So yes, there have - and there have been other projects. For example, we did an information paper on sovereign citizens."[217]

In the days leading up to a joint session of Congress, where every national law enforcement agency was on high alert, the head of intelligence for the USCP was assigning research papers with absolutely no nexus to the immediate threat environment.

USCP INTELLIGENCE FAILURES ARE DIRECTLY TO BLAME FOR THE LACK OF PREPAREDNESS ON JANUARY 6, 2021.

C. Farnam undermined IICD analysts and downplayed important intelligence to USCP leadership.

During that period, IICD analysts completed a first special event assessment on December 16, 2020 and updated the assessment on three occasions to include new information.[218] The December 16 assessment concluded there was "NO social media indications for specific threats or concerning comments directed at the Joint Session of Congress."[219]

Analysts told investigators they were not advised about how to prepare for the imminent Joint Session until mid-December 2020. In one case, an intelligence assessment update for the event was tasked to an analyst on December 21, 2020, and the analyst only had 12 hours to complete it. The hastily prepared assessment was not published. The analyst testified:

> **Question:**
> So, in the lead up to, let's say mid-December, Capitol Police knows the Joint Session is happening. . . . In those weeks leading up to it, were [you] given any information?
>
> **Answer:**
> Zero information. Zero. Even the day of, we were given zero information.[220]
>
> * * *
>
> When it came time for the Joint Session, I was tasked, December 21st, to write an assessment on the Joint Session. . . . So, I did not see that until the 22nd when I logged in in the morning. I started writing it, she called me the next day, I think the next morning, and asked where the assessment was. And I said, "I'm still researching it." She goes, "I need it by lunch time."
>
> So, I had, basically had 12 hours to totally research this whole thing, which I would have been working on for at least a month. Totally research it and write it. And I admit that was awful assessment because I did not have the time to put into it, and research it. And I was not familiar with the subject matter.

USCP INTELLIGENCE FAILURES ARE DIRECTLY TO BLAME FOR THE LACK OF PREPAREDNESS ON JANUARY 6, 2021.

Question:

Right.

Answer:

So I wrote that. As far as I know that was not published. The next week, [USCP analyst] was tasked with writing an assessment on the Joint Session. [The analyst was] not told that I had written one the previous week. But [the analyst] wrote an assessment. As far as I know, that was not published.[221]

The next document shared by IICD was produced on December 21, 2020.[222] The report signaled concerns about the Joint Session for the first time. The December 21 IICD Report attached a map of the tunnels of the Capitol complex that appeared online and indicated protesters could be "carrying firearms during the protest" and could "confront members of Congress."[223]

Senate Committee investigators interviewed Yogananda Pittman, who was serving as Assistant Chief in charge of the Protective Intelligence Operation on January 6, 2021.[224] According to the Senate Report, "The December 21 IICD [intelligence] Report attached a map of the Capitol campus that was posted to the blog and noted: 'several comments promote confronting members of Congress and carrying firearms during the protest.'"[225]

This report was labeled 21-TD-159.[226] Pittman told Senate investigators, "this report was distributed only to "command staff," including the deputy chiefs and assistant chiefs."[227]

Capitol police officers—according to Pittman—would have received that report. But USCP sources testified to investigators they never saw it, and never received it.[228] According to the officers, Pittman lied to Senate investigators. One USCP source testified:

Answer:

And everybody, every deputy chief, knew they didn't get this email and that everybody had been lied to. So, like I said, that's when people started like, did you get that? No. Did you get it? And they're like, no.

USCP INTELLIGENCE FAILURES ARE DIRECTLY TO BLAME FOR THE LACK OF PREPAREDNESS ON JANUARY 6, 2021.

Question:
So you've confirmed with everyone that no one got that email?

Answer:
One hundred percent. Yeah. Everybody's certain of that.[229]

Additionally, Farnam confirmed in her interview with investigators that the report was not shared with officers.[230] A whistleblower similarly told House and Senate leaders that Pittman lied about whether her officers were prepared in advance for the brutality they faced on January 6.[231] A USCP source told investigators that the entire USCP force acknowledges that Pittman did not testify truthfully to the Senate, and accordingly it will be difficult to trust her to lead and protect the rank-and-file.[232]

IICD sent out several additional assessments after December 21, most of which were reproductions of previous information that did not indicate violence was a concern.[233]

The final Special Assessment was shared on January 3, 2021.[234] This was the first assessment that mentioned Congress was the target of violence. The document, however, did not include that important fact in the "Bottom Line Up Front" portion on the first page, but rather buried it toward the end of the fifteen-page assessment.[235]

Regarding the placement of that key portion of the assessment, the USCP Inspector General found, if one "does not read the [January 3 Special Assessment] in its entirety, they could draw an inaccurate conclusion since the [Bottom Line Up Front section] is not consistent with the rest of the document."[236]

Jack Donohue and Julie Farnam tasked two analysts to write the final Special Assessment.[237] Throughout mid to late-December, they drafted three versions and received edits from Donohue.[238] The portion that stated Congress was the target of violence, however, was written by Farnam.[239]

The source of the intelligence that led Farnam to conclude the Capitol was a target is unclear. Indeed, Farnam testified that she drafted the final assessment.[240]

USCP INTELLIGENCE FAILURES ARE DIRECTLY TO BLAME FOR THE LACK OF PREPAREDNESS ON JANUARY 6, 2021.

The documents and testimony create the appearance that Farnam used the work of the analysts to cobble together the assessment to send to USCP leadership. One analyst described the process of writing the assessment during an interview with investigators.

The analysts testified:

Answer:

January 3rd, Julie [Farnam] writes the assessment. She took a little bit from mine, basically talking about how the Joint Session would work, the background, and the list of demonstrations that I'd found at that point, and she put that in there. And she took a little bit from [the other analyst's].

And she composed the assessment that was published prior to 1/6, I think it was the 3rd or the 4th. And she put the BLUF in there, the bottom line up front, that did not say anything about violence. I, we didn't get that until I would say, either late on the 4th or the 5th, when Jack Donohue sent it to us, after it had been published to other people.

Question:

So, you're saying that her threat assessment that she sent out on the 3rd, was sent to you by Jack Donohue on the 4th or the 5th?

Answer:

Yes.

Question:

And did it include threats, possible violence in that version?

Answer:

It was the version that everybody's talking about. I did not, when I read that document, and I've talked to the other analysts, they had the same impression from me, that that document tell anybody that it was, to expect violence that we experienced. There was nothing in there.

USCP INTELLIGENCE FAILURES ARE DIRECTLY TO BLAME FOR THE LACK OF PREPAREDNESS ON JANUARY 6, 2021.

Answer:
When I wrote my first assessment and I had all these demonstrations listed, she came back to me and said, "Well, these are all different groups, but there's probably only going to be five, so we only need to be concerned about five demonstrations." I said, "Those 40 demonstrations are people coming from all over the country, that tells us something, that's important to know that we have 5 people coming from Alaska, and 20 people for Minnesota, and 500 coming from Maryland," and that's important information, and she did not see it that way.

She just thought it's five main demonstrations and these other groups are just going to join in those. I disagreed, but, like I said, she never really published [my version of the assessment] with her list, she copied and pasted, I believe, some of it, into the assessment.[241]

On this issue, Farnam testified she was not concerned about the permits because "COVID protocols" only allowed 50 people per permit.[242] This statement shows a staggering lack of awareness and concern, especially in light of more than a year of massive protests throughout the country where "COVID protocols" were ignored.

Farnam testified that she and her team do not bear responsibility for what happened on January 6, 2021.[243] She said "[IICD] provided leadership with information that it was going to be violent, that Congress was going to be targeted, that extremists would be there, that there were going to be thousands of protesters, and that intelligence was not operationalized."[244]

Farnam is relying on the portion of the January 3 Special Event Assessment that she sent up the chain of command that included the lines: "protestors have indicated they plan to be armed" and that "Unlike previous protests . . . Congress itself is the target on the 6th."[245] However, there was no relevant or underlying information along these lines in prior assessments, nor in three subsequent Daily Intelligence Reports. Farnam admitted she should "have given those reports more attention on January 4, 5, and 6."[246]

USCP INTELLIGENCE FAILURES ARE DIRECTLY TO BLAME FOR THE LACK OF PREPAREDNESS ON JANUARY 6, 2021.

But Farnam also testified that concerns about the possibility of violence during the Joint Session developed much earlier, to late December.[247] She stated:

> **Because remember, you know, the MAGA 2 March was December 12th, and so January 6 wasn't even a thing until after December 12th. I didn't learn of it until, you know, mid-December sometime, and it wasn't until we got closer to the end part of December right around the holidays that we really started to see things pick up.[248]**

Farnam's testimony about the timeline of her concerns about the possibility of violence at the Capitol during the Joint Session is contradictory and alarming. The Joint Session to count the electoral votes was the focus of much national news in the weeks leading up to January 6, 2021.[249] The Joint Session is a constitutionally mandated process; even under normal circumstances, the USCP's preparation for a joint session of Congress should be a high priority for the department's chief intelligence officer far in advance of the event.[250]

Farnam testified the first indicators of violence came around December 21, 2020. She stated, "around that time is when we started to see more worrisome intelligence coming in."[251] Farnam appears to be referencing the December 21 IICD report that mentioned the Capitol tunnels and the likelihood that protesters could be armed.

But, according to her testimony, those concerns were neutralized by her confidence that COVID protocols only allowed 50 people per permit. Farnam further testified that she learned there would be thousands of people at the Ellipse rally and the Freedom Plaza rally around mid to late December.[252] Even that information did not seem to register with Farnam, in terms of the heightened potential for violence during the Joint Session. Farnam testified that, even after learning about the larger-than-expected rallies in mid to late December, she did not develop concerns until "right around the new year." She stated:

> **Question:**
> You also told CBS you said, "I knew things were not going to be good that day." Did you know that on January 3rd? Did you know that December 21st?

USCP INTELLIGENCE FAILURES ARE DIRECTLY TO BLAME FOR THE LACK OF PREPAREDNESS ON JANUARY 6, 2021.

Question:
When did you know things were going to be bad?

Answer:
I'd say right around the new year. [253]

So, while experienced and tenured analysts were alerting Farnam to the need to consider the fact that multiple events were coalescing in the vicinity of the Capitol, Farnam continued to incorporate "COVID protocols" into her overall threat assessment. The results were catastrophic.

While Farnam stated in a televised interview with CBS as a part of an anniversary special that she "knew things were not going to be good that day," the day before the Joint Session, the entire team of intelligence officers of the USCP attended a mandatory training. [254] When pressed about why she would send her staff to a training when she knew there could be violence the next day, she responded, "because the violence wasn't happening on the 5th." [255]

That day, the FBI's Norfolk Field Office shared a Situational Information Report regarding online discussions of potential violence at the Capitol on January 6, 2021. [256] One analyst described how USCP failed to register the FBI's warning. The analyst testified:

> **[W]e were so fragmented and nobody was really focused on that. If this would have been under a previous manager, Norm, it would have been all hands on deck as soon as we got inklings that there was going to be violence everybody would have been working on it, that would have been our focus. Instead we were being fragmented and moved around, so, yes, I could see where that information did not make it to the officers. . . . [W]hatever information they passed to Julie was not passed to us. We didn't know about that information from the Norfolk office until after the event when it came out in the press is when we learned about it. [257]**

USCP INTELLIGENCE FAILURES ARE DIRECTLY TO BLAME FOR THE LACK OF PREPAREDNESS ON JANUARY 6, 2021.

Such failures had consequences department-wide. The fifth USCP OIG flash report stated:

> **Many of the officers interviewed stated they received very little or no intelligence about events planned for January 6, 2021, or that it would be any different than previous MAGA events. For example, one officer stated they did not receive any intelligence that day and that social media was a better source of information because it forecasted the intensity and the number of people.**[258]

The documents and testimony show the abrupt changes to the processes for gathering and disseminating intelligence within IICD and USCP in late 2020 were counterproductive and ill-conceived in advance of a high-profile event. The processes that Farnam inherited had kept the Capitol safe for years. Farnam's decision to overhaul the intelligence division amidst mounting evidence that various groups intended to direct violence at the Capitol during the upcoming Joint Session left the USCP under-prepared to perform its mission.

D. IICD leadership reorganized the division to gather more intelligence on Members of Congress, staff, and constituents to the detriment of preparing for the Joint Session.

One of IICD's responsibilities is to produce Congressional Event Assessments (CEAs), which are assessments requested by the Dignitary Protection Division, Members of Congress, or House or Senate Sergeants at Arms. These assessments are specific to events that Members hold in their district or events outside of Washington, D.C. that they wish to have reviewed by USCP analysts. Julie Farnam overhauled the protocols for CEAs.

Analysts interviewed for this investigation explained that a Member of Congress is encouraged to submit a list of all participants and the location of the event to the Sergeant at Arms. The Sergeant at Arms then transfers that information to IICD to run a check.[259] This check, also known as LECOR (Law Enforcement Coordination), is an open-source check on all the names provided by the Member of Congress via the Sergeant at Arms.[260] Analysts assessed any derogatory information identified during the LECOR.[261] USCP Chief Manger testified that USCP does not run record checks or criminal history checks.[262]

USCP INTELLIGENCE FAILURES ARE DIRECTLY TO BLAME FOR THE LACK OF PREPAREDNESS ON JANUARY 6, 2021.

He stated: "if there is nothing derogatory or nothing of concern, the information is not kept. If it—if there is something of concern, it's put in the assessment."[263]

House Sergeant at Arms William Walker also testified about the process for vetting the people who meet with Members of Congress. He stated:

> [Y]ou're going to -- you name the place. You're going to meet with people there. Who's going to be there? Are they predisposed to violence? Do they have a criminal history? Are they violent? Do they have -- are they somebody that's made a threat against you? Just want to understand who's around you.[264]

One analyst, however, described the process in more specific terms. The analyst testified that USCP also ran checks on Members of Congress and Senators, congressional staff, and donors. The analyst stated:

> **Answer:**
> If we, when the form that we get from the Sergeant of Arms House or Senate, if they list Members that are, and other Members that are attending, staffers that may be attending, who they're meeting with. If there's names in there, we have to research them, and we have to go back and see -- look at their social media accounts.
>
> As an example, this summer I had numerous meetings. [Republican Senator], he was meeting with donors, and I had to background the donors. I had to go and look at their social media accounts, which most of them were elderly and didn't have social media accounts.
>
> **Question:**
> Right.
>
> **Answer:**
> I had to look at their residence. I had to see who owned the residence and where it was located. And most of them, they know, the Members know where they're going.

USCP INTELLIGENCE FAILURES ARE DIRECTLY TO BLAME FOR THE LACK OF PREPAREDNESS ON JANUARY 6, 2021.

In response to questions about researching a donor's house, Walker testified: "I would hope a Member would want to know who has proximity to him, who's within arm's reach, who can reach out and cause alarm. I would hope."[265] But Walker did not answer whether Members knew that USCP was conducting such research on the people whose names they submitted to the Sergeant at Arms. According to a copy of the template that Farnam created, analysts were directed to review the people meeting privately and publicly with members, and to describe "the backgrounds of the participants (other than [Members of Congress]) and attendees, if known."[266]

Indeed, the security value of such research is further undermined by the fact that the resultant case file was not reviewed by Dignitary Protection agents. A USCP source testified:

> **Question:**
> So, these new requirements, did Ms. Farnam create a form so that you have to basically fill it out, so you're asked the same questions from every person, or how would these instructions relate to you?
>
> **Answer:**
> She made a new form, and she sent it out, and it was, it would have the heading and she would put in parentheses what to put in there.
>
> **Question:**
> [S]o the form gets filled out. You do the work that is requested of you, and you send it up. And, you don't know what happens to it next, is that fair?
>
> **Answer:**
> No. That's fair.
>
> **Question:**
> And so how do you learn about whether or not all the information you've gathered and all this work that you've done is going to somewhere useful, or if it's going into a file or a somewhere else?

USCP INTELLIGENCE FAILURES ARE DIRECTLY TO BLAME FOR THE LACK OF PREPAREDNESS ON JANUARY 6, 2021.

Answer:
Word of mouth.

Question:
Word of mouth. And so, have you heard instances in which you know you did a big project on an event and then later you learned that the people who were actually working that event didn't ever have the benefit of your work?

Answer:
Yes, we've heard back from some of the DPD agents, the Dignitary Protection agents, that they have not seen what we wrote. So, it, I don't know where this information's going, and I feel like we're almost spinning our wheels. [267]

If the information collected against private citizens exercising their constitutional rights with respect to meeting Members of Congress is not in fact used for security purposes by the officers responsible for securing those meetings, then the purpose of the program and the scope of the information collected needs to be reviewed.

Similar concerns were covered in a January 2022 story in Politico, which stated:

POLITICO

As a general practice, Farnam directed analysts to search for any information about event attendees, including donors and staff, "that would cast a member in a negative light," according to one person familiar with the workings of the department's intelligence office. This included searching for information about mayors, Hill staff, and state legislators. [268]

USCP INTELLIGENCE FAILURES ARE DIRECTLY TO BLAME FOR THE LACK OF PREPAREDNESS ON JANUARY 6, 2021.

On January 25, 2022, Republicans wrote a letter to the Capitol Police Board, demanding answers on these allegations.[269] Chief Manger responded on January 27 in a letter detailing IICD's processes and asked the USCP OIG "to review the USCP's programs related to these security assessments . . ."[270]

It is important to note that the USCP OIG as a matter of course does not review claims made by media outlets—it only reviews those by whistleblowers, Congressional stakeholders, or the USCP Chief of Police. This is reflected in the USCP OIG's May 2022 report on IICD, which does not address the claims in the Politico article. The report states in the methodology section that OIG "could not benchmark IICD processes and procedures against other protective agencies' processes," meaning the report fails to address the key allegations at stake in this matter.[271] The specific constitutional and civil liberties concerns raised in the Politico story therefore remain unresolved by USCP and unaddressed by the USCP OIG, and they are reaffirmed by this investigation.

E. USCP leadership doubled down on their failed management approach and retaliated against officers and analysts who raised concerns.

Since the analysts in the open-source section came forward to speak with investigators and filed official complaints with the USCP Office of Inspector General, they have been retaliated against and, in some cases been terminated.

For example, one analyst testified that he was asked to participate in the Select Committee's investigation by USCP, and then written up for participating. He testified:

> **Answer:**
> I was contacted by [Capitol Police attorney]. And she was the one who notified me that the January 6 Committee was interested in conducting an interview. She asked for some available times, and she was the one who actually scheduled the interview. In my response to her I requested that, you know, Capitol Police . . . not be present for the interview due to my complaints of ongoing retaliation, discrimination, harassment by my supervisor, Ms. Farnam. She said that was fine. I conducted the interview with the January 6 Committee. There was no Capitol Police presence.

USCP INTELLIGENCE FAILURES ARE DIRECTLY TO BLAME FOR THE LACK OF PREPAREDNESS ON JANUARY 6, 2021.

Answer:

I found out on Monday in speaking with [Capitol Police attorney] that she had contacted Ms. Farnam about my meeting with the committee. She would not say what they talked about. And then when I pressed her and asked about my request not to notify my supervisor because of ongoing retaliation, she said that -- she said, I cannot make demands of the Inspector General. I said, of course not. I understand. I am making a request. Can you just acknowledge if my request will be upheld or not? And her comment was that she cannot speak anymore about my request for the Capitol Police not to be notified.

Question:

Did she give you a reason why she notified Ms. Farnam?

Answer:

She did not. She said she could not talk about her conversation at all other than she had a conversation. A few hours after that, I was contacted by Ms. Farnam, and we had a teleconference where she issued me a CP-550, which is an administrative document. In the document, she cited mismanagement of my time and prioritization of resource -- of casework. Because during the day, she had given me two assessments to complete. But due to my two-and-a-half hours with the interview, I was only able to complete one assessment.

So that was her justification for issuing me the administrative write-up.[272]

Analysts testified that Farnam intentionally created a toxic environment. According to witnesses, Farnam's strategy was to "create stress" in order to assess the adaptability and resilience of IICD analysts. One analyst testified:

Answer:

She also said that she wanted to create stress, and so she could evaluate the adaptability of the analysts. Yet she has put in an email that there was a method to her madness, as she put it. Those are her words. That she wanted to see which analysts could adapt to new and difficult assignments.

USCP INTELLIGENCE FAILURES ARE DIRECTLY TO BLAME FOR THE LACK OF PREPAREDNESS ON JANUARY 6, 2021.

Question:
So she told you that she intentionally created stress to see if you were able to adapt under stressful situations?

Answer:
Yes. She said this in an all-hands-on teleconference with everybody in the division. Because we had been sending so many complaints to our supervisors. Inspector Schneider was also on the call, and Chief Gallagher was on the call, and they, you know --

Question:
Which are her supervisors, correct?

Answer:
Correct. And they were on the call because they had been receiving so many complaints of us just gross mismanagement. We were essentially -- the military term is combat ineffective. **We were not able to properly perform our jobs under the current conditions.** [273]

In response to this testimony, Chief Manger stated: "Well, certainly that's not the way I would want a supervisor to conduct their day-to-day activities." [274] Manger also stated that he would not tolerate retaliation: "I will not tolerate people being mistreated, discriminated against, retaliated against. I have been doing this a long time. And there is -- there are times when I have, in fact, taken action because I felt that someone was mistreated or someone was retaliated against. I won't tolerate it." [275] But in consideration of Farnam's endeavor to disassemble the open-source section of IICD, reassign analysts to new tasks they were not trained to do, and purposefully create a stressful environment, Manger remained satisfied with the department's direction. He said:

USCP INTELLIGENCE FAILURES ARE DIRECTLY TO BLAME FOR THE LACK OF PREPAREDNESS ON JANUARY 6, 2021.

Answer:

We are far and away much better. . . . I am not kept up at night by, oh, my God, could this -- you know, could intelligence be the problem again? We need to stay on top of it. Make no mistake. It's not like I don't think about it. I do. But I know that with the improvements we have made, that these improvements will be sustained for years to come.

Question:

Okay. So it's safe to say that you are satisfied with the changes that have been made in intelligence?

Answer:

There is more work to be -- yes, I am.

The analyst sources who testified and assisted this investigation were subsequently separated from the USCP.

F. USCP is withholding an internal report that confirmed many of the concerns raised by analysts and officers who testified to investigators.

U.S. Capitol Police completed its After-Action Report on June 4, 2021.

Notably, this report was not shared with the Capitol Police Board and was only shared with the USCP Inspector General after he concluded his investigation. Further, USCP has not officially provided the After-Action Report to either Republicans or Democrats on the Committee on House Administration despite bipartisan requests, and they have yet even to inform the Committee that the After-Action Report is complete as of the writing of this report. The After-Action Report made several findings related to the Intelligence Division that align with the testimony of analysts who participated in this investigation. The After-Action report was provided to investigators through concerned whistleblowers. The findings state:

73

USCP INTELLIGENCE FAILURES ARE DIRECTLY TO BLAME FOR THE LACK OF PREPAREDNESS ON JANUARY 6, 2021.

1. Intelligence products must be updated and disseminated for appropriate planning and officer readiness.
2. Individuals with the most experience extrapolating open source material were not tasked with reviewing social media to glean intel related to the even.
3. IICD was urged in an email, to be sure that the Bottom Line Up Front (BLUF) was on all their documents. This is put into an assessment to express urgency or concerns.
4. The intelligence briefing that Hazardous Incident Response Division (HIRD) received differed from the official intelligence reports, causing confusion in preparation, postings, and overall response at the Capitol.
5. Minimal updates were provided by units in the field assigned to monitor demonstration activity prior to the arrival on U.S. Capitol Grounds.[276]

The findings make clear that USCP's After-Action Report confirmed what several analysts shared during transcribed interviews with investigators and tends to confirm the department's dysfunction under the management of Julie Farnam. Farnam ignored these findings and the analysts who raised concerns were terminated by USCP.

RECOMMENDATIONS

This investigation found that the events of January 6, 2021 revealed structural and operational failures by the Capitol Police Board. To prevent a similar situation from happening again, and to ensure USCP is prepared to respond in case it does, it is imperative that Congress embraces the original intent of the Board: the separation of security decisions from politics. For that reason, the Board's structure must be reformed.

To do so effectively, distance must be created between congressional leadership and USCP so law enforcement and intelligence experts are making security decisions, not politicians. The Board must also demonstrate a commitment to functioning as an oversight entity, not an entity carrying out the partisan demands of the Speaker. The Board needs to drive transparency and accountability at USCP through proactive oversight with long-term objectives in mind, rather than taking a passive and opaque role beholden to the political winds of the day. The recommendations made below are intended to acknowledge the important role the Board plays, the structural failures that contributed to January 6, and the path forward for Capitol security.

A. Make the Capitol Police Board more transparent

There are necessary changes unrelated to the Board's structure that must be made to ensure transparency and accountability at USCP and the Board. These changes could take place with or without changes to the Board's structure to correct longstanding issues.

COMPEL THE BOARD TO SEND MEETING MINUTES TO THE RELEVANT OVERSIGHT COMMITTEES

Require more consistency and timeliness from the Board in communication and sending meeting minutes to oversight entities – There has been a consistent lack of transparency from the Board regarding security decisions, recommendation implementation, timelines, and other oversight related requests. Due to pressure from House Republicans, the Board has taken steps to improve transparency, including providing the oversight committees copies of their Manual of Procedures, the Board's monthly meeting minutes, and creating the Capitol Police Board Fora.

RECOMMENDATIONS

To increase oversight and accountability, it is important that the Board submit minutes to the House Committee on House Administration, the Senate Committee on Rules and Administration, and House and Senate leadership offices in a consistent and timely manner.

REQUIRE THE BOARD TO REGULARLY APPEAR BEFORE THE RELEVANT OVERSIGHT COMMITTEES

The Board, in its entirety, has not met with any Senate or House committees since 1946. When asked to do so post-January 6, 2021, the newly appointed Senate Sergeant at Arms refused to participate. The Board members who did participate in CHA's oversight hearing deflected requests for information, stating they could not make such a commitment without the full Board's approval. The Board should be required to meet annually before a Joint Committee of Senate Rules and CHA, with the expectation that requests for information from the Joint Committee shall be answered, fully.

PROVIDE ADDITIONAL RESOURCES FOR THE CAPITOL POLICE BOARD TO PROFESSIONALIZE ITS SUPPORT STAFF

Administrative functions of the Board are often conducted by borrowed staff from the House Sergeant at Arms and Architect of the Capitol offices, used to supplement the needs of Board members. It is important to consider providing additional executive staff specifically to serve the Board to professionalize the Board's functions, establish clear points of contacts, and ensure proper documentation and record keeping. There should also be consideration for more staff on the oversight committees with experience in policing and protective forces.[277] The Board should also be compelled to meet before either committee at the call of the Chair. It is important that these committees have the resources to attract experienced security analysts capable of overseeing USCP and the Board. This will also inspire confidence from the Board in the expertise of the relevant oversight entities. Despite a statutory change after the events of January 6, 2021 requiring this to occur every Congress, no oversight hearing has been scheduled by the Democrat-majorities in the House or Senate.

RECOMMENDATIONS

CLEARLY DEFINE AND LIMIT THE BOARD'S AUTHORITY

The Board's structure and responsibilities are an "anomaly" relative to peer security entities, according to the 2017 GAO report. The Board's direct role in the day-to-day operations of the USCP hinders USCP's mission and, as witnessed on January 6, dangerously handicaps USCP's function. The Board's focus should be limited to long-term strategic thinking and overseeing USCP's budget. The Board also needs to prioritize its oversight responsibilities in relation to tracking and implementing the USCP IG's recommendations.

MAKE THE INSPECTOR GENERAL INDEPENDENT FROM THE BOARD

The USCP IG has testified before CHA four times since January 6, 2021. Though thorough in his investigations of the security shortcomings on January 6, the IG is limited and conflicted in his oversight role of the Board. His refusal to answer basic questions about the Board's responsibilities and operations demonstrates that the IG is not able to conduct audits of the security posture of the Capitol when the Board holds much of the decision-making responsibilities and directs the actions of the IG. For this reason, we recommend that the authority to hire and remove the USCP IG be shifted to the relevant oversight committees, with three-fourths of the Chairs and Ranking Members of those committees sufficient to approve any personnel actions. The Inspector General's budget should also be independent from the Board.

B. Reform the structure of the Capitol Police Board

The structure of the Board needs to change. It cannot be left to the two Sergeants at Arms to make all security decisions for the Board. Adding members from outside of the USCP and of the political chain of command would ensure less political influence and introduce new perspectives to USCP and the Board. Further, the Board needs to shift away from making day-to-day management decisions for USCP to overseeing its operations and ensuring coordination between various stakeholders, both on and off the Hill.

RECOMMENDATIONS

These proposals aim to balance the various considerations above to address the findings contained herein related to the politicization of security decisions and the USCP's overall level of professionalism.

ADD TWO NEW MEMBERS TO THE CAPITOL POLICE BOARD

Two new members should be added to the Board whose full-time job will be oversight of USCP, long-term strategic planning, and identifying industry best practices. These new members should be appointed to staggered terms of four years. The appointing authorities should prioritize members with pre-existing relationships at relevant Executive Branch departments, including the Department of Defense, Department of Homeland Security, and Department of Justice, who can facilitate a direct line to those departments in circumstances like those on January 6, 2021. Prior experience as either a chief of police, police commissioner, or security director of a prominent state or federal protection agency should also be prioritized. Given its hybrid nature, USCP would benefit from protective and policing experience on the Board.

REPLACE THE CHIEF OF POLICE WITH THE COMMISSIONER ON THE BOARD

Currently, the chief of police's role on the Board creates a conflict of interest. They are tasked with overseeing the department of which they are in charge. This position should be replaced by the newly installed commissioner who will liaise with the Board and the chief of police to inform the oversight goals of the Board. It will also make a clear division of oversight between the Board and the Department.

APPENDIX

Thursday, December 3

- House Sergeant at Arms staff receive an intelligence report from USCP IICD that reflects an event at the Capitol on January 6. The report includes time, date, and location information for the event: "Donald Your [sic] Fired March on DC." It is labeled as an anti-Trump event that could draw counter demonstrators, and it has 2 people listed as going and 12 more that are interested. The Level of Probability for civil disobedience/arrests is listed at "highly improbable."[278] House Sergeant at Arms Paul Irving receives a separate daily briefing from his staff that does not include information for January.[279]

Saturday, December 5

- Jamie Fleet, a shared staffer on Speaker Pelosi's and the staff director for the Committee on House Administration, texts Irving with the contact information of a large metropolitan area's police chief and mentions the name of a member-elect to Congress from that city. Fleet then states, "If you let me know when you connect I'll close loop with np."[280]

Sunday, December 6

- Irving sends an update to Jamie Fleet, saying, "Just spoke with [Police Chief] and established contact; also spoke with Chief Sund who will liaise with the . . . Police Chief and ensure all threats and security issues pertaining to the Member-elect is transmitted to the USCP."[281]

Tuesday, December 8

- Terri McCullough, Speaker Pelosi's Chief of Staff, texts Irving, "Paul would you be available sometime between 12-3 for a meeting or call with Speaker?" Irving agrees to the meeting and they schedule a time.[282]

APPENDIX

Wednesday, December 9

- Jamie Fleet texts Irving, to ask if he has touched base with the previously mentioned Member, saying, "NP hosting a pick up lunch today and most members will be by."[283]
- Irving texts Fleet, saying, "Just FYI, we have a good plan for the issue you raised regarding opening day."[284]

Friday, December 11

- House Assistant Sergeant at Arms relayed concerns with renovations being made to an alternative Chamber space on Campus. The Assistant Sergeant at Arms notes that "[i]f the project were to proceed as scheduled, it would require CAO to make additional equipment purchases and install and configure it for use. This will take several weeks to months after the completion of the AOC project. . . This leaves the House with no viable on-site alternate chamber option during two highly important event [sic] – Opening Day of the 117th and Joint Session for Electoral Count." Later in the day he follows up to say that Jamie Fleet weighed in on the situation, agreeing that the work should be postponed.[285]
- Terri McCullough emails a Sergeant at Arms staffer to request a meeting. The email states, "...[W]e have had a number of internal discussions about choreography and safety for the Opening day and electoral college events. Can we get together with you and your team early next week to map out what we think we need given the complexities presented?" They schedule a meeting for the following Tuesday at 10am.[286]

Monday, December 14

- 9:39am: Irving asks one of his staffers to call him. The staffer says he is available to talk. The next text references Jamie Fleet.[287]

Tuesday, December 15

- Irving meets with members of Speaker Pelosi's and Committee on House Administration's Democratic staff.[288]
- A draft order for the temporary restriction of access to House Office Buildings from January 3 to January 6 is passed along to Irving from a HSAA staffer. The draft states that " . . . such closing is necessary assure [sic] the security or safety of persons in the House Office Buildings, or the preservation of peace or good order, and securing the House Office Buildings Building [sic] from defacement, and for the protection of public property therein . . . "[289]

APPENDIX

- Irving texts Jamie Fleet, asking, "Should we send the draft Opening Session [Dear Colleague] to just you (and Terri [McCullough]), or to the group that was on the call this am?" Jamie tells him "That group." [290]

Wednesday, December 16

- House Sergeant at Arms staff receive a Daily Intelligence Report with information for the first time referencing a Pro-Trump rally. The report says that on January 6 "Patriot Party and Pat King - Patriots United March on Congress" will be at the Capitol with the exact location to be determined. It says that as Congress meets to count electoral votes, " . . . they must know that We The People will not sit idly by without a full accounting for every legal vote cast on November 3rd. March for Election Integrity. March for the Constitution. March to Save America. Come to Washington and meet us at the base of the Capitol." It says that the group had listed on their social media page 49 people attending and 294 interested in the event at the time of the report. The Level of Probability listed for acts of civil disobedience/arrests is listed as "highly improbable." [291] This information was not included in the intelligence briefing sent to Irving. [292]
- Without further context, then-Chief of U.S. Capitol Police Steven Sund texts Irving to say, "Not in favor of a [redacted] fence." Irving responds, "Copy. You'll need to provide adequate posting nonetheless, but I know the AOC wants [redacted]. I'd ask that your staff work closely with the AOC staff to find a mutually agreeable [redacted] decision." [293]

Thursday, December 17

- In a personal exchange with a friend, Irving says, "...when your text came in I was consumed with Opening Day and Electoral College logistics. The week of January 3 will be very challenging." [294]

Friday, December 18

- USCP circulates to staff of the Senate Sergeant at Arms, House Sergeant at Arms, and the Architect of the Capitol an invitation to join a meeting on January 5 to discuss plans for the Inauguration along with stakeholders from across the National Capitol Region. [295]
- Irving texts Jamie Fleet, saying, "First draft models coming to you from Erik [Speranza with House Sergeant at Arms]. Prepared to discuss anytime (either direct with Erik or also with me and Tim)." [296]

APPENDIX

Sunday, December 20

- Jamie Fleet texts Irving to ask when he is back in town from the holidays, saying, "Sent you a teams thing for meeti [sic] tomorrow on special opening day issues." [297]

Monday, December 21

- Irving receives a Daily Intelligence Report, mentioning the Million MAGA March, Woman for a Great America-50+ Days of Blessing, and Ali Alexander's Stop the Steal protests for the first time. Very little details are provided here, but the Level of Probability for acts of civil disobedience/arrests is listed as "remote" for each demonstration. [298]

Monday, December 28

- Irving receives a Daily Intelligence Report with 17 new protests planned for January 6 around the Capitol campus. Most of them are Pro-Trump, but two are Anti-Trump groups, both reference being there in "force." The likelihood of civil disobedience/arrests is listed as "improbable" for both. For the other 15 protests, likelihoods of disobedience/arrests range from remote to improbable. [299]

Tuesday, December 29

- Chief Sund requests to set up a call with Irving. Irving responds that he is available. Then, he says, "Be careful that [a prominent Democratic member of Congress] doesn't ask you to have your officers pick her up from home. The answer is NO [emphasis added by Irving]." [300]
- Assistant Sergeant at Arms Tim Blodgett sends a draft front office schedule for January 3 – January 8. In order to comply with Office of the Attending Physician guidance on maintaining social distancing, their schedule has half of the staff working in the office and the other half in telework or scheduled leave. [301]

Wednesday, December 30

- Irving receives a Daily Intelligence Report that now includes 27 protests on the day, the overwhelming majority of which are pro-Trump. All the protests continue to list the likelihood of civil disobedience/arrests ranging from "remote" to "improbable." [302]

APPENDIX

Thursday, December 31

- Irving receives a Daily Intelligence Report that now has 22 protests on the day. All of the protests continue to list the likelihood of civil disobedience/arrests ranging from "remote" to "improbable." [303]

Saturday, January 2

- Irving texts Jamie Fleet, saying, he " . . . spoke with Terri [McCullough] about vandalism issue (will provide greater coverage of the home and researching prosecution options, Federal and State, and will be getting back to her), and also spoke about the 6th – a draft [Dear Colleague] coming your way on Member safety and security for the day." [304]

Sunday, January 3

- Irving accepts a meeting with USCP for an intelligence briefing regarding January 6 from 11:00am-12:00pm. [305]
- House Sergeant at Arms office circulates a draft e-Dear Colleague to be sent out to members of Congress and Congressional staffers for First Amendment activities taking place at the Capitol on January 6. In the draft, they along with USCP encourage members and staff to arrive early, park in garages, and use alternative routes to walk through the protest areas. The recommendations mention that there will be additional police on campus that day and provides contact information for when they are on campus. The draft also includes information about how official business visitors are to access the Capitol. [306]
- 6:53pm: Without further context, Jamie Fleet directs Irving via text, "You should come to the floor" and "Officers might come quick." Irving responds "En route." [307]

Monday, January 4

- 7:49am: Irving texts a House Sergeant at Arms staffer to request a call, saying, "I have an idea about the [Dear Colleague] language we spoke about last night and thought I'd share it before you do any heavy drafting." [308]
- Jamie Fleet reaches out to Chief Sund and Irving to set up a meeting with their offices and Committee on House Administration Chairperson Lofgren where they can discuss the security arrangements for January 6. The email states that the "brief should include a discussion of USCP staffing levels, coordination with other department, and your determination to extend (or not) the perimeter around the Capitol (e.g. using jersey barriers to keep folks off the plaza etc.)." [309]

APPENDIX

- 11:35am: Irving texts Fleet, saying, "[Representative Rodney] Davis also wants a briefing; can we do a joint or do you prefer separate? Either way obviously works." Fleet did not respond. [310]
- Irving receives the USCP IICD "Special Event Assessment" dated January 3, and it includes the intelligence analysis, saying that "Congress itself is the target on the 6." [311]
- Irving receives a Daily Intelligence Report that now has 23 protests on January 6. All the protests continue to list the likelihood of civil disobedience/arrests ranging from "remote" to "improbable." [312]
- 2:30pm-3:00pm: Irving meets with the Speaker's office to discuss the Electoral College Count. [313]
- House Sergeant at Arms staffer sends an updated draft of the e-Dear Colleague regarding security information for January 6 to Terri McCullough and Jamie Fleet. They request "any edits, comments, or concerns." [314]
  - Terri McCullough responds shortly after with edits. She suggests clarifying parking language, timing of events, and edits to the language regarding official business visitors. Given that they are not allowing guests to the Capitol (as they previously discussed according to her) "it sends a mixed signal..." [315]
  - The House Sergeant at Arms staffers agree to the changes proposed. [316]
  - The House Sergeant at Arms incorporates the edits suggested by McCullough and says they will send it out. [317]
- 4:28pm: Irving texts Jamie Fleet, saying, "We're making Terri [McCullough]'s edits to the electoral college and if you don't mind, I'll send it to you and Jen [Daulby, Committee on House Administration, Republican staff director] as a heads up, so please act surprised." Fleet responds, "I'm startled!" [318]
- The e-Dear Colleague with the suggested edits is sent out to the House. [319]
- The Office of the House Sergeant at Arms receives notice of a threat against a senior Republican Senator from USCP Investigations Division. [320]

Tuesday, January 5

- 7:16am: Irving sends to Chief Sund a web link to an article discussing the Metropolitan Police Department of D.C.'s (MPD) arrest of the Proud Boys leader. Irving says, " . . . just thought I'd send it along to let you know the story broke. And always interesting how the media gets information that we may not necessarily get from our sources . . ." [321]

APPENDIX

- 8:15am: Jamie Fleet, sends edits to a proposed timeline of events sent by Speaker Pelosi's director of floor operations, Keith Stern. Irving and Terri McCullough, are included on the email. [322]

- 8:30am-9:00am: House and Senate Sergeants at Arms and representatives from USCP meet to conduct a walkthrough for the Electoral College Joint Session.[323] Terri McCullough, and other Democratic staffers from the Majority Leader and Democratic Cloakroom were invited to attend. No Republicans are listed in the invitation.[324]

- 9:18am: A Sergeant at Arms staffer sends a draft copy of a Dear Colleague to Terri McCullough to be sent out to members and staff regarding security concerns with the upcoming Electoral College Count, and requests feedback on what needs to be changed. [325]

- 10:00am-10:30am: Irving meets via video conference with Committee on House Administration Chairperson Zoe Lofgren regarding security arrangements for Wednesday's Joint Session.[326]

- 10:02am: The House Sergeant at Arms staff receives a Daily Intelligence Report that now has 24 protests listed on January 6. All the protests continue to list the likelihood of civil disobedience/arrests ranging from "remote" to "improbable." [327]

- 10:14am: Dr. Brian Monahan, the Attending Physician, responds to the Floor and Operations Manager in the Sergeant at Arms Office to ask if there is a "plan to limit the maximum number of people that can be in the Chamber" for the Joint Session. He also suggests, "Perhaps we could be more prescriptive about people attending who fail to wear a mask or more stringent language barring children and anyone other than the Member in the interest of reducing the people in the chamber." The Floor and Operations Manager responds, saying, "Yes; the plan is to limit Senate/House staff – Speaker's office is coordinating this as we speak. We will also do as we do for voting, and do everything in groups of no more than 72 at a time on the Floor. We will direct overflow Members to the Gallery." [328]

- 10:20am: Irving receives notice of another threat against the same senior Republican Senator from USCP Investigations Division.[329]

APPENDIX

- 11:22am: An Architect of the Capitol staffer sends to the Capitol Police Board and their assistants a note informing them that they are prepared with "normal assets: and increased staff". It is unclear what the context of this email is. [330]

- 11:50am: Terri McCullough responds to the e-Dear Colleague regarding January 6 security concerns with two suggestions:
  - "To Members are encouraged to remain in their offices can we add unless or until they are called to vote?" [sic]
  - "Also can we add similar staff guidance (except no voting)?" [331]

- 12:00pm-1:00pm: Irving joins a meeting hosted by Chief Sund with law enforcement partners to discuss the Inauguration. [332]

- 12:03pm: House Sergeant at Arms staffer sends to Jamie Fleet a draft Dear Colleague detailing road closures for January 6. He requests "edits, comments or concerns." [333]

- 2:20pm: House Sergeant at Arms Director of Protocol and Chamber Operations responds to proposed edits from the Speaker's staff director, saying they will verify with Dr. Monahan regarding the proposed edits and send another draft. [334]

- 12:32pm: Jamie Fleet says the street closure Dear Colleague "looks good." [335]

- 12:32pm: House Sergeant at Arms Director of Protocol and Chamber Operations sends an updated version of the COVID procedures Dear Colleague with the changes Terri McCullough suggested to Irving. [336]

- 12:40pm: Jamie Fleet sends a follow-up email from his earlier message regarding the street closures Dear Colleague, saying, "Wait a minute. How are members who drive themselves going to get to the garage? Will there be check points. [sic] We need to discuss that in the note." [337]

- 12:42pm: Without further context, the House Sergeant at Arms Director of Protocol and Chamber Operations sends an updated copy of the COVID protocols Dear Colleague to Irving. [338]

- 1:15pm-1:45pm: Irving schedules a walk-through with House Sergeant at Arms staff for the Electoral College. [339]

- 1:30pm: Terri McCullough reaches out to Irving to thank a House Sergeant at Arms staffer who "masterfully handled a difficult situation with two members refusing to wear masks on the floor." She says he should expect Mr. Clyburn and the Speaker "may be coming to you at some point to discuss additional support for the staff in these situations..." [340]

APPENDIX

- 1:32pm: A House Sergeant at Arms staffer reaches out to Irving to let him know they scheduled a 2:30pm walkthrough for January 6 with staff. It also references another walkthrough just prior to that with Senate Sergeant at Arms, Mike Stenger.[341]
- 1:56pm: The House Sergeant at Arms Director of Protocol and Chamber Operations emails Dr. Monahan an updated version of the COVID protocols Dear Colleague.[342]
- 1:59pm: House Sergeant at Arms staffer emails Jamie Fleet with the updated road closures Dear Colleague with Fleet's recommended changes incorporated.[343]
    - 2:05pm: Jamie Fleet responds, saying, "Good."[344]
    - 2:27pm: The House Sergeant at Arms staffer sends out to both Jamie Fleet and Jen Daulby, Republican staff director on House Administration Committee, the street closures Dear Colleague, requesting feedback from both parties as though he had not already received feedback from the Democrats.[345]
- 2:30pm-3:00pm: Irving conducts a walkthrough of the evacuation plan for the Joint Session of Congress.[346]
- 2:55pm: Chief Sund requests a conference call meeting with the other Capitol Police Board members to discuss moving bike racks on campus intended for crowd control.[347]
    - 3:43pm: Chief Sund circulates a new perimeter, seemingly in follow-up to their conversation.[348]
    - 3:56pm: Paul Irving agrees with the new perimeter.[349]
- 4:00pm-4:30pm: Irving meets with Appropriations - Legislative Branch Subcommittee Chairman Tim Ryan to discuss threats.[350]
- 4:00pm: COVID procedures Dear Colleague is disseminated by the House Sergeant at Arms.[351]
- 4:02pm: Chief Sund in a group text with the two Sergeants at Arms informs them that "MPD just locked up 2 with weapons 9th and Constitution."[352]
- 4:05pm: Terri McCullough texts Irving, saying she is stuck in a meeting and will call about the next day soon.[353]
- 4:26pm: Road Closures Dear Colleague is disseminated by the House Sergeant at Arms.[354]
- 4:57pm: A Democratic staffer from the Appropriations - Legislative Branch Subcommittee Majority sends an email questioning how close National Guard troops deployed for traffic control purposes will be in relation to the Capitol complex, saying, "I only ask to be ahead of any members who might question a photo or live tv shot that shows National Guard with the Capitol dome in the backdrop."[355]

APPENDIX

- 4:57pm: Irving responds to the Democrat Appropriations staffer, saying, "Good talking with you this evening. My cell is [phone number redacted] and my desk is [phone number redacted]. Don't hesitate to call with any questions or issues (everyone else does!)." [356]
- 5:40pm: Terri McCullough texts Irving, saying, "Paul – when is a good time to talk about this afternoon and the floor tomorrow." They agree to speak at 6:15pm. [357]
- 6:17pm: Terri McCullough messages Irving, requesting to push back their 6:30pm meeting to 6:45pm, due to her being stuck in another meeting. [358]
  - 6:18pm: Paul Irving agrees to push back the meeting. [359]
- 6:20pm: Irving sends a text to Michael Stenger, Senate Sergeant at Arms, asking, "Are you making any notification regarding the Intel that I'm told is going public?" Stenger responds, "I am under the impression that it has been deemed aspirational." Irving responds, "Agree, all good." They do not text again until January 11th. [360]
- 6:37-6:40pm: Terri McCullough and Paul Irving coordinate to call at 6:45pm. [361]
- 6:52pm: House Sergeant at Arms staffer sends around a CBS tweet, stating that "the FBI and FAA are looking into a breach of air traffic control frequencies after a threat was made about flying a plane into the Capitol on January 6. [362]
- 7:07pm: A staffer for Senator Schumer's Office emails Chief Sund, copying the House and Senate Sergeants at Arms and McConnell's staff on the email, requesting guidance on how to advise Senate Leadership. [363]
- 7:24pm: Chief Sund responds, saying they are investigating, along with federal partners, and they "have no information deeming this as credible." [364]
- 7:50pm: Wyndee Parker, Speaker Pelosi's National Security Advisor, reaches out to Irving, requesting more information on the aviation threat. Irving responds shortly after, saying he will call her. [365]
- 8:31pm: A staffer in Senator McConnell's Office responds to the chain of emails regarding the aviation threat, saying "I must observe there is collective concern from the Congressional leadership about learning about this threat reporting from the media rather than from USCP or SAA. We are also concerned that timely notification may not have been made to USCP and SAA and are making inquiries with respective federal agencies. Even if it is not a credible threat, we want to ensure the systems we have in place are appropriate." [366]

APPENDIX

- 8:55pm: Deputy Chief Sean Gallagher emails House Sergeant at Arms, notifying them that online groups found maps of the Capitol tunnel system, and they were planning to find and utilize them to confront members of Congress. Further, there was an uptick in messaging of "groups intentions of forming a perimeter around the campus . . . from 0600-1000 hours in order to block all MOC's from getting inside our perimeter to the Buildings with spots identified for direct action." [367]

- 9:06pm: In response to the chain of emails between Chief Sund and Senate Leadership staff, Irving sends a note to a senior HSAA staffer, "The Chief has taken [Architect of the Capitol] Brett [Blanton]'s place. Unbelievable." [368]

- 9:10pm: AOC Chief Security Officer emails Blanton, informing him of changes being made to the bike rack perimeter. [369]

- 9:09pm: The senior HSAA staffer responds, "Oh good god. And of course [Senator McConnell's staffer] has nothing to do right now except stir everyone up." [370]

- 9:09pm: Irving forwards the chain of emails between Chief Sund and Senate Leadership staff to Michael Stenger, "Nice Leadership on your side." [371]

- 9:12pm: Irving emails the senior HSAA staffer separately, stating, "Just FYI, I briefed Terri, Jamie and Wyndee. So, they're all good. They got it before the story broke. Stenger told me earlier he wasn't going to tell anyone, and this is the result. I love Mike, but same story, the SSAA doesn't get it: brief Leadership in advance of the story" in response to the senior HSAA staffer's message." [372]

- 9:14pm: The senior HSAA staffer responds to Irving, "Exactly though I think [Senator McConnell's staffer] would still get spun up." [373]

- 9:16pm: Paul responds to the senior HSAA staffer's earlier message, "Yeah, I guess you're right. But, at least Stenger doesn't care, so...who does? Phenomenal!" [374]

- 9:21pm: Blanton responds to Hasberry, saying "Val, This seems absolutely illogical. It removes a zone of defense. If you find out a logical impetus for the change, let me know ASAP. I'll make calls to the board if necessary." [375]

- 10:29pm: Tim Blodgett emails Paul Irving to inform him that three House security officers were exposed to COVID-19, and they are unable to get tested until the next day, meaning they are unavailable for service for January 6. Additionally, this results in their SCIF being unavailable for January 6. [376]

APPENDIX

- 11:37pm: A staffer in Senator McConnell's Office relays his frustration to Chief Sund on the lack of forthcoming information on intelligence. He states, "Although it is encouraging USCP was made aware of this threat reporting last night, it raises more questions about why the Joint Congressional Leadership only became aware of it through the news media." He goes on to request further information as to when both Sergeants at Arms were notified, why Joint Congressional Leadership were not notified, and what protocols are in place for sharing such information with Leadership.[377]
- 10:49pm: Tim Blodgett emails Paul Irving, saying the SCIF will be cleaned in time for the next day.[378]

Wednesday, January 6
- 7:46am: Chief Sund sends a text to the two Sergeants at Arms, saying "MPD reporting approximately 10,000 already in line for the ellipse event." The ellipse event was the rally planned where President Trump would be speaking. This is the only text exchange sent in the group chat until 8:52pm.[379]
- 8:06am: Call from Admiral Brian Monahan for 3 minutes.[380]
- 8:13am: The director of protocol and chamber operations emails Paul Irving to inform him that Speaker Pelosi's director of operations " . . . coordinated with House and Senate Leadership to agree on recommended [underlined by author] numbers for the Floor . . . " and how they plan to control numbers on the Floor.[381]
- 9:00am: A House Sergeant at Arms staffer circulates a map of the permitted demonstrations around the Capitol for that day. They received the map from USCP Command Center. This map was initially sent to AOC's Command Center, Senate Sergeant at Arms, and House Sergeant at Arms. The map depicts the Capitol surrounded by five of those protests with another protest by the Russell Senate Office Building. This is the first time that the map arrives in Irving's inbox.[382]
- 9:04am: Hasberry responds to Blanton's email from January 5, saying "The racks were moved after a meeting with between Paul Irving and Chief Sund. They walked the site on Monday and the concern by the HSAA was that the House side was not as protected as the Senate." She mentions later in the email, "There are several historical factors on why AOC has not been included in these decisions that I can discuss with you later. I will continue working to improve the coordination and input.[383]
- 9:10am: Irving receives the "[IICD] Situational Report 01/06/2021." It includes 25 protests, and one protest that is no longer listed on social media."[384]

APPENDIX

- 9:32am: The director of research and data at the US Sentencing Commission sends a note to Paul, saying "Good luck today. Stay safe." [385]
- 9:35am: Call from Chief Sund for 2 minutes. [386]
- 9:45am: USCP liaison in the HSAA office sends to the HSAA office, "USCP responding to report of individuals with a propane cooker on the North CVC Walkway." [387]
  - 9:50am: the individuals are sent away. [388]
- 9:51am: Speaker Pelosi's National Security Advisor sends a note to Irving, saying "USCP notified on Monday but you weren't notified until late Tuesday afternoon. FBI provided a very detailed timeline that showed very active USCP engagement on Monday. In fact USCP was alerted as late as 7 pm Monday. That was good but you as HSAA should have been given a heads up much earlier." It is not clear without further context what this message is referencing, but it appears to be regarding the airplane threat. [389]
  - Irving responds, saying "Definitely agree; I wasn't notified until Erik briefed me at about 4 p.m. yesterday. He got notified by the PO, not USCP. The Chief called me around 6 p.m. to inform me (and I told him that I had just been notified by the PO). I was unaware that the USCP had the information on Monday. I'll speak with the Chief about this." [390]
  - 10:13am: Speaker Pelosi's National Security Advisor responds, "Thanks. Again the Monday night and Early Tuesday unclassified timeline FBI laid out to us re: USCP contact and engagement is extensive." [391]
- 10:00am: Call to Luke Murry, National Security Advisor for Republican Leader Kevin McCarthy, for 1 minute (possibly unanswered). [392]
- 10:20am: Terri McCullough requests to connect with Irving. Irving says he can meet "shortly." [393]
- 10:26am: Call to Luke Murry for 10 minutes. [394]
- 10:32am: Admiral Brian Monahan sends suggested language to Irving, saying "The Attending Physician has determined that the number of people present on the House floor is in excess of the predetermined coronavirus risk reduction requirement The [sic] Attending Physician requires that operations be temporarily paused to permit excess personnel to leave the House floor at which time operations can be resumed." [395]
- 10:36am: Irving is alerted that "Radio reports about a black pickup with Trump flags and reports of a catapult in the bed. They were initially stopped earlier coming over the 14th Street Bridge and released. USCP stopping the vehicle, I believe at S. Capitol and E. Streets, SW, out of caution to interview the driver verify what is in fact in the bed of the truck." [396]

APPENDIX

- 10:48am: Call to Senate Sergeant at Arms Stenger for 6 minutes. [397]
- HSAA counsel sends language to Irving, "Melding House OGC's advice and OAP's advice" provided at 10:32am. [398]
    - 10:50: Irving sends the updated language to Admiral Monahan, adding that he is consulting the Parliamentarian. [399]
    - 10:54am: Admiral Monahan responds, asking "What would be the enforcement mechanisms for noncompliance in response to invoking the statutory authority?" [400]
- 10:51am: Irving receives a Daily Intelligence Report. There are 26 protests at the Capitol noted for the day, 17 are explicitly Pro-Trump, 3 are Anti-Trump, and the rest are either religious or interest-group gatherings appearing to be right-leaning. All the protests continue to list the likelihood of civil disobedience/arrests ranging from "remote" to "improbable." [401]
- 11:01am: HSAA office is alerted that "A group of approximately 200-300 of the "Proud Boys" is reportedly coming up the Mall, headed toward the Capitol. This group is known for civil disobedience and occasional outright violence." [402]
- 11:02am: HSAA staffer forwards to Irving an update from Sean Gallagher of USCP from 11:01am. The update was sent to staffers from House and Senate Sergeants at Arms. It includes the following:
    - "Our intelligence assessment that we sent on Monday stands as accurate for today. We have been inundated with posts from_social media showing pictures of weapons, anti-Congress and anti-police statements_. We have given all of our operational teams the most updated information for their situational awareness. We have all hands on deck for USCP and all of our teams are operational."
    - "This entire crowd will be marching to the Capitol at the conclusion of POTUS' speech. Almost every speaker so far has engaged the crowd to "get up to the Capitol" or "Let's go storm the Capitol" as soon as the event is over. Numerous subjects are wearing body armor, ballistic helmets, military grade backpacks and carrying radio equipment. Our partner agents will be assisting with this massive march to the Capitol and our SOD and CDU teams are aware of the march. It is anticipated that POTUS will arrive somewhere after 1100/1130 and depart at 1215. The crowd would start marching after that to the Capitol." [403]
- 11:05am: Irving forwards the question about enforcement from Admiral Monahan to his staff. [404]
    - 11:06am: HSAA counsel responds with a link to US Code, saying that quarantine violators will be subject to a fine, imposed by the House Sergeant at Arms. [405]

APPENDIX

- 11:11am: HSAA office is alerted that "'Proud Boys' group has arrived to Capitol grounds. They are lining up by the Reflecting Pool at the moment." [406]
- 11:12am: Irving responds to Admiral Monahan, saying "I'll check with the Parliamentarian and attorneys, but the enforcement mechanism would probably be recessing subject to the call of the chair (to clear and clean the chamber and re-establish the appropriate number)." [407]
- 11:13am: HSAA is alerted that "USCP responding to reports of a disruptive individual on the Senate Egg." [408]
- 11:19am: HSAA is alerted that "'Proud Boys' group has taken Garfield Circle." [409]
- 11:20am: Admiral Monahan responds, saying "Thanks." [410]
- 11:25am: HSAA is alerted that "'Proud Boys' walking up SW Drive." [411]
- 11:34am: HSAA is alerted that "'Proud Boys' also walking up Constitution toward the East Front. They and other groups are converging on the East Front at this time." [412]
- 12:06pm: Call from Irving to Admiral Monahan for 1 minute (possibly unanswered). [413]
- 12:13pm: Irving emails Brian Monahan that "Terri [McCullough] does not want us to use the "Q" word, so we're going to soften it. Please call when you get a moment. Thanks." The "Q" word in question is quarantine. [414]
- 12:16-12:17pm: There is confusion between the House General Counsel, Douglas Letter, and HSAA office whether Admiral Monahan signed a quarantine order. Speaker Pelosi's staff is consulted for clarification over email. [415]
- 12:19pm: HSAA is alerted for the first time of a breach to the fence. "USCP responding to the communications tower area near 2nd and Constitution NW. A group of demonstrators has breached the fence in order to use the porta-potty." [416]
- 12:19pm: Terri McCullough, Speaker Pelosi's Chief of Staff, responds to the question of whether the Attending Physician signed a quarantine order, simply saying "no." [417]
- 12:23pm: Staffer in HSAA emails Irving, Admiral Monahan and HSAA counsel with new proposed language for what to say in the event of a capacity issue on the House Floor. [418]
- 12:26pm: Speaker Pelosi's National Security Advisor forwards a tweet to Paul Irving, saying "Trump announces he's going to Capitol Hill this afternoon. "We are going to cheer on our brave senators and congressmen and women. We're probably not going to be cheering for some of them . . ." [419]
    - 12:27pm: Irving forwards this email to his deputy. [420]
    - 12:27pm: Irving responds, saying "Thanks; have NOT heard this, I'll contact USSS off-line and see what I can find out." [421]

APPENDIX

- 12:27pm: A staffer in Senator Schumer's office sends a message to Chief Sund with House and Senate Leadership staffers from both sides of the aisle and the two Sergeants at Arms, requesting crowd estimates.[422]
  - Chief Sund responds, "Looks like a couple thousand on Capitol grounds and a very large event down at the Ellipse and Washington Monument Grounds. We are currently monitoring several thousand marching down Pennsylvania Avenue towards the Capitol now." [423]
- 12:30pm: Call from Terri McCullough for 1 minute (possibly unanswered).[424]
- 12:32pm: HSAA is alerted for the first time of a taser being heard (but unconfirmed) at the Senate Egg. [425]
- 12:33pm: Call to Terri McCullough for 2 minutes.[426]
- 12:44pm: HSAA is alerted that "POTUS speech has concluded. Groups are headed our way. The group currently walking up Penn Ave is estimated to be 10,000."[427]
- 12:45pm: Chief Sund emails Brett Blanton, Michael Stenger, and Paul Irving that "The President has completed his speech at the Ellipse and the large group at the event is preparing to march to the Capitol." [428]
- 12:45 pm Irving calls Chief Sund for 1 minute (possibly unanswered).[429]
- 12:47pm: HSAA is alerted to a radio report "of a suspicious package behind the RNC" that initial reports say is "a black pipe 'bomb looking' device with timer/wires attached to it." [430]
- 12:57pm: HSAA is alerted that "Group has pushed through the bike racks on the West Front from Peace and Garfield. Grounds only. Locking down South Door, Law Library Door, North Door, Lower Terrace Door out of precaution." [431]
- 12:58pm: Call to Chief Sund for 1 minute (possibly unanswered). [432]
- 12:59pm: HSAA staffer messages Irving, saying "barricades are breached. Protesters are approaching the inaugural stand," "UsCp [sic] are engaging," and "Protesters holding at base of stand but have accessed press platform." Shortly after, she texts him about a medical incident at West Dome, and "Will communicate further on other device." She then states, "I have your things snd [sic] secured your office." [433]
- 1:01pm: HSAA is alerted that "Demonstrators starting to swarm the Inaugural stage. Not compliant. Calling all available hands to Upper West Terrace to an elevated position."[434]
- 1:02pm: HSAA is alerted that the Madison Building is being evacuated due to the bomb threat.[435]

APPENDIX

- 1:08pm: HSAA staffer send Irving a note, saying "Protesters now on press risers talk of using less lethal." [436]
- 1:09pm: HSAA is alerted to reports of a bomb threat at DNC. [437]
- 1:12pm: HSAA is alerted that the Cannon House Office Building is being evacuated due to the bomb threat. [438]
- 1:15pm: HSAA staff receives from IICD a tweet by a Washington Post journalist, saying "Protestors are charging toward the Captiol [sic] steps. Some tried to scale the construction structures and have been tackled by police. They want to enter the building and are making attempts at intervals. Capitol police trying to hold them back." [439]
- 1:16pm: A staffer in Senator Schumer's office requests an update from Chief Sund on whether the President is coming to the Hill, and whether folks have broken through the barricade. [440]
- 1:21pm: HSAA staff are told that USCP and MPD are holding the line at the Lower West Terrace on the West Front." [441]
- 1:25pm: A staffer in Senator McConnell's office requests information on the evacuation of Madison and Cannon. [442]
  - Senator Schumer's staffer responds with a tweet, saying "Trump supporters have breached the Capitol building, tearing down 4 layers of security fencing and are attempting to occupy the building — fighting federal police who are overrun." [443]
- 1:28pm: Call from Chief Sund for 3 minutes. [444]
- 1:30pm: Call from Don Kellaher from the House Sergeant at Arms office for 2 minutes. [445]
- 1:32pm: Call to Jamie Fleet for 1 minute (possibly unanswered). [446]
- 1:33pm: Irving texts Jamie Fleet, saying, "Tried to call with an update. Call anytime." [447]
- 1:33pm: Jamie Fleet returns call for 1 minute (possibly unanswered or ended early due to next call). [448]
- 1:33pm: HSAA staff are alerted that "Individuals throwing projectiles and arguing with officers on the line. [449]
- 1:34pm: Call from Chief Sund for 1 minute (possibly unanswered). [450]
- 1:37pm: HSAA staff are alerted that "Demonstrators deploying some kind of flash-bangs or smoke bombs down on the LWT. Not sure of the specific nature of the smoke from the cameras yet." [451]
- 1:39pm: Chief Sund responds to the chain email with Stenger, Irving, and the Senate and House staffers, saying "Cannon will be doing internal relocations. Madison evacuating due to suspicious package." [452]

APPENDIX

- 1:40pm: HSAA staff are told that USCP is calling for a decontamination tent to be set up. [453]
- 1:43pm: A HSAA staffer emails Irving to tell him protestors are "tearing down scaffolding." [454]
  - 1:45pm: The same staffer informs him that there is a large breach to the East Front. [455]
- 1:45pm: Call from Chief Sund for 4 minutes. [456]
- 1:49pm: Two calls with Terri McCullough for 3 minutes. [457]
- 1:50pm: HSAA staff are informed that a "Shelter in Place" notice for the House Office Buildings is about to be issued." [458]
- 1:51pm: HSAA staff are informed that "Demonstrators starting [sic] to mount the stairs toward the Upper West Terrace." [459]
- 1:51pm: Back-to-back 1-minute calls with Blodgett. [460]
- 2:00 – 2:07 pm Two calls to HSAA and two calls from Chief Sund. It appears the calls from Sund went unanswered. [461]
- 2:00pm: HSAA staff are informed that "Demonstrators how [sic] breaching the East Front. Capitol is going to be placed in lockdown shortly." [462]
- 2:08pm: HSAA staff are informed that "Demonstrators flooded the East Steps en masse and are attempting to enter the Rotunda Door. Demonstrators also on the West steps trying to enter the LWT Door." [463]
- 2:09pm: HSAA staff are informed that the "Campus is on full lockdown." [464]
- 2:14pm: Call from Jamie Fleet for 1 minute (possibly unanswered). [465]
- 2:14pm: Brian Ebert from U.S. Secret Service texts Irving, saying, "Wanted you to know that Director has reached out to Sund to offer any/all Service support. SAs and officers rolling now." Irving responds shortly after, "Thank you. We've been breached and could use the help." [466]
- 2:15pm: Call from Blodgett for 2 minutes. [467]
- 2:20pm: HSAA staff are informed that reinforcements are gearing up. [468]
- 2:22pm: Call from Sean Gallagher for 4 minutes. [469]
- 2:25pm: HSAA staff are informed that "...we have essentially lost our exterior perimeter. Units being called inside the Capitol. MPD and other LE assets maintaining presence outside. HDS detonating both the packages at the DNC and RNC." [470]
- 2:27pm: Call from Stenger for 4 minutes. [471]
- 2:30pm: Call from Terri McCullough for 1 minute (possibly unanswered). [472]
- 2:31pm: Both Chambers being evacuated. Tear gas being deployed at the Rotunda Door. [473]

APPENDIX

- 2:34pm: Call from Kim Campbell from the House Sergeant at Arms office for 2 minutes.[474]
- 2:39pm: HSAA staff are informed that "Demonstrators are attempting to enter the House Chamber."[475]
- 2:41pm: Call from Stenger for 2 minutes.[476]
- 2:44pm: HSAA staff are informed that "Shots fired on the House Floor."[477]
- 2:51pm: Call to Stenger for 1 minute (possibly unanswered).[478]
- 2:53pm: HSAA staff are informed that there are "reports of officer down in the Dirksen subway."[479]
- 2:57pm: Call from Jamie Fleet for 1 minute (possibly unanswered).[480]
- 2:57pm: Call from Kim Campbell for 2 minutes.[481]
- 3:02pm: Call from Kim Campbell for 1 minute (possibly unanswered).[482]
- 3:07pm: Call to Jamie Fleet for 1 minute (possibly unanswered).[483]
- 3:08pm: Irving texts Jamie Fleet, saying, "No text, please re-send." Fleet responds, "Didn't go thru" and "So command center is saying guard on the way?" Irving responds, "Yes, they indicate the.National [sic] Guard is on the way." After some confusion, Irving says, "They are en route. I'm told some leadership from the NG have shown up at the USCP Command Post but not the troops yet."[484]
- 3:09pm: Call to Bob Dohr, Chief Operations Officer for the House Sergeant at Arms for 2 minutes.[485]
- 3:26pm: Call to Bob Dohr for 2 minutes.[486]
- 3:27pm: Call from Stenger for 1 minute (possibly unanswered).[487]
- 3:28pm: Call from Jamie Fleet for 2 minutes.[488]
- 3:30pm: Call to Bob Dohr for 1 minute (possibly unanswered).[489]
- 3:31pm: Call to Jamie Fleet for 2 minutes.[490]
- 3:34pm: Call from Jamie Fleet for 2 minutes.[491]
- 3:36pm: Call to Bob Dohr for 2 minutes.[492]
- 3:38pm: Call to Jamie Fleet for 1 minute (possibly unanswered).[493]
- 3:43pm: Call to Terri McCullough for 5 minutes.[494]
- 3:55pm: HSAA staff are informed that "CNN reporting that the protestors breached the Speaker's Office."[495]
- 4:02pm: A staffer for Rep. Tim Ryan on the Appropriations, Legislative Branch Subcommittee emails leadership of HSAA, USCP, Clerk's office, Speaker Pelosi' office, and House Administration's Democratic staff that "All video of today's events needs to be preserved, and after the protestors are removed, an investigation needs to begin immediately."[496]

APPENDIX

- 4:09pm: Call from Chief Sund for 4 minutes.[497]
- 4:13pm: Call to Stenger for 2 minutes.[498]
- 4:28pm: Call from unknown number ending in 2911 for 10 minutes. 702 area code (Fairfax, VA).[499]
- 4:32pm: Jamie Fleet texts Irving to say, "when it's safe to do if drew [sic] and I can get a look in the chamber that would be helpful" followed by "only when it's safe to do so" and "Drew and I are outside [the Committee on House Administration's main office] for whoever wants to get us. Thank you." Irving responds, "Officers en route", "Are you be [sic] route yet?", "En route?" Fleet affirms they are on their way.[500]
- 4:33pm: Jamie Fleet opens a group chat between Paul Irving, Erik Speranza (HSAA), and himself, asking for estimates on how long it will take for various locations to again be operational.[501]
- 4:34pm: An update to the HSAA staff notes that most of the Capitol is cleared of demonstrators and the House Chamber is secured.[502]
- 4:41pm: Call to Jamie Fleet for 1 minute (possibly unanswered).[503]
- 4:46pm: Call to Don Kellaher for 5 minutes.[504]
- 4:56pm: Call from Chief Sund for 2 minutes.[505]
- 5:08pm: HSAA staff are informed that "CDU assets are preparing to push demonstrators down the West Front steps. [USCP Deputy Chief] Eric Waldow also just called for a platoon to try to re-establish an East Front perimeter."[506]
- 5:18pm: Call from Sund for 3 minutes.[507]
- 5:19pm: HSAA Counsel texts Irving to inform him that "[Representative Rodney] Davis has indicated a desire to inspect the chamber, if possible."[508]
- 5:21pm: Call to Erik Speranza for 2 minutes.[509]
- 5:28pm: Call from Stenger for 4 minutes.[510]
- 5:30pm: Erik Speranza texts Irving, requesting to set up a call between Cheryl Johnson, the Clerk of the House, Catherine Szpindor, the Chief Administrative Officer of the House, and him.[511]
- 5:44pm: Call to Chief Sund for 5 minutes.[512]
- 5:41pm: Calls (2) from Chief Sund lasting 5 minutes.[513]
- 5:57pm: "National Guard is on the West Front assisting with pushing the perimeter back to at least 1st Street. East Front perimeter mostly re-established at this time. Capitol Building interior has been confirmed CLEAR of demonstrators. Both Chambers being inspected right now for damage and to determine whether we will reconvene on-site or possibly at the alternate location. We should have that information within an hour."[514]

APPENDIX

- 5:59pm: Call from Jamie Fleet for 2 minutes.[515]
- 6:12pm: Call from Emily Berret (Speaker's then-Director of Operations) for 9 minutes.[516]
- 6:13pm: Call to Sund for 8 minutes (this was a 3-way phone call with Berret).[517]
- 6:22pm: Call to Stenger for 2 minutes.[518]
- 6:23pm: Brian Ebert, Chief of Staff of the US Secret Service, messages Irving to let him know that "the Service has been getting pinged by Executive Branch leadership about assisting you with erecting fencing around perimeter of Capitol [sic]" and offers to "support in any way." [519]
- 6:29pm: HSAA staff are alerted that "Perimeter has been pushed back to the 1st Streets, between Independence and Constitution. USCP conducting exterior sweeps at this time. House Egg/SE Drive are clear." [520]
- 6:30pm: Call to Jamie Fleet for 2 minutes. [521]
- 6:32pm: Call from Stenger for 1 minute (possibly unanswered).[522]
- 6:34pm: Call to Terri McCullough for 2 minutes.[523]
- 6:42pm: Call to Stenger for 2 minutes.[524]
- 6:53pm: Call to Terri McCullough for 2 minutes. [525]
- 6:59pm: Assistant Sergeant at Arms sends to Irving language for reconvening the House. [526]
- 7:10pm: Irving sends his first email since 12:37pm. It is an email to Jamie Fleet with plans on how to reconvene the House, along with the language from the Assistant Sergeant at Arms. [527]
- 7:22pm: Call to Jamie Fleet for 2 minutes.[528]
- 7:25pm: Call to Jen Daulby, Republican Staff Director of the Committee on House Administration, for 2 minutes.[529]
- 7:25pm: Irving emails Terri McCullough and Jamie Fleet to inform them that "The Capitol is secure and we can resume activity in the Chamber at your discretion." [530]
    - 7:29pm: McCullough responds to say, "Paul we need to talk to you about limiting members on the floor for the remainder of the proceedings." [531]
- 7:57 - 8:22pm: Calls (3) with Sund totaling 8 minutes.[532]
- 8:37pm: Call from Stenger for 2 minutes.[533]
- 8:41pm: Call from Brian Monahan for 2 minutes.[534]
- 8:52pm: Chief Sund texts the two Sergeants at Arms to say "MPD went to 12 hour shift and all days off cancelled." [535]

APPENDIX

- 9:46pm: HSAA counsel forwards an article of statements made by prominent Democrats, including Rep. Tim Ryan saying "there were some strategic mistakes from the very beginning" and "I think it's pretty clear that there's going to be a number of people who are going to be without employment very, very soon." [536]
- 10:09pm: The Capitol Police Board executive assistant emails the members of the Capitol Police Board to inform them that they need to sign two Board Orders for approval. One is an emergency order beginning at 6:00pm on January 6 to be in place for 48 hours. The other is a curfew for the building, beginning at 6:00pm on January 6 until 6:00am on January 22nd. [537]
- 10:21pm: Jamie Fleet requests of Irving, "Can you come to floor?" Irving does not respond. [538]
- 10:48pm: Call to Stenger for 6 minutes. [539]
- 11:06pm: Michael Stenger says, "ok," in response to the CPB orders. [540]
- 11:12pm: HSAA staffer approves CPB orders on behalf of Paul Irving. [541]
- 11:23pm: AOC staffer approves CPB orders on behalf of J. Brett Blanton. [542]
- 11:27pm: Call from Ted Daniel for 1 minute (possibly unanswered). [543]
- 11:33pm: Republican staff director of the Committee on House Administration emails Irving to request follow-up on a man who claimed he was in the building who witnessed Ashli Babbitt's shooting and was conducting the interview from his hotel room. [544]
- 11:58pm: HSAA staffer responds, saying they have forwarded to MPD. [545]
- 11:58pm: USCP General Counsel emails the HSAA staffer, saying a recent call was "Brutal. Ryan is furious. Sen. Murphy less so but not happy." [546]

Thursday, January 7

- 3:41am: Chief Sund sends to the members of the Capitol Police Board a draft statement regarding the events of January 6. [547]
- 7:16am: AOC staffer emails HSAA staff to let them know that they are conducting a full assessment of the damage caused by January 6. [548]
- 9:13am: Wyndee Parker, Speaker Pelosi's National Security Advisor emails Irving, saying "Paul, I hope you are hanging in there. Lots to discuss. An item for right now: Pls ensure that rigorous ID checks are being done today. We are getting reports from people entering the plaza and building that it isn't happening this morning." [549]
- 9:19am: Terri McCullough emails Irving to ask if his team has been in touch with Transportation Security Administration for enhanced security for members traveling to their districts." [550]

APPENDIX

- 10:49am: Chief Sund circulates to all Capitol Police Board members the US Capitol Police statement on January 6 for their review.[551]
- 11:17am: A HSAA staffer emails Irving to let him know that Jamie Fleet "is looking for arrest number comparisons for other Capitol grounds protests especially BLM protests." Irving responds, inquiring if USCP is handling it.[552]
- 11:31am: Irving forwards Wyndee Parker's request for "rigorous ID checks" to Chief Sund, saying, "please ensure ID checks are happening." Chief Sund agrees to the request shortly after.[553]
- 4:10pm: Following the announcement of Irving's resignation, a HSAA staffer sends him an email frustrated by the events from January 6 and the fallout, stating:
  - "For the Speaker's knee-jerk reaction to yesterday's unprecedented event (and God knows how Congress lives for its knee-jerk reactions and to hell with future consequences . . .). To immediately call for your resignation . . . after you have been denied again and again by Appropriations for proper security outfitting of the Capitol (and I WROTE several of those testimonies, dangit) . . . and to blame you personally because our department was doing the best they could with what they had and our comparatively small department size and limited officer resources . . . and because other agencies stepped in to assist just a fraction too late . . . again, for Congress to demand your resignation is spectacularly unjust, unfair, and unwarranted. This is not your fault. Or Sund's fault. If anything, Appropriations should be hung out to dry. (In fact, our biggest Approps whiner [I will not name names, but you know who I mean] is now demanding a personal escort to and from her DC residence to the Capitol and to the airport and anywhere else she wants to go). Frankly, you would have been damn well within your rights to authorize lethal force as soon as the Capitol Doors were breached. But the point may be made that, of the two evils, we chose to protect human lives in the end. And the Capitol is still standing. A little worse for wear, maybe . . . but still standing. THAT is a successful day, in my book."[554]
- 6:07pm: Irving sends an updated security notice to be sent out from his office to House offices, to Jamie Fleet for his review.[555]
- A HSAA staffer texts Irving a link to a tweet with footage of USCP officers allowing protesters through the East gate. Irving responds, "Not surprising. They breached too fast."[556]

APPENDIX

- Following a message of condolence from a friend, Irving responds, "Please know that I'm fine. I'm so at peace with my career and the decisions we made last night. You know this town, you live by the sword, you die by the sword." [557]
- Responding to a message of condolence, Irving says, "These high profile DC jobs have their pros and cons. And this is one of the cons. Taking the hit; so it goes. I'm at peace with my career and life, and I feel we made all the right decisions at the time." [558]

Friday, January 8

- Irving texts with a HSAA staffer, expresses frustration with the USCP officers who let protestors into the building, saying "the video of the officers letting the protesters in absolutely outrageous [sic] me." He goes on to say, "It's incredulous. I just don't trust the USCP anymore. Not my issues now, but beware. Either incompetence or blatant sympathy to Trump." [559]
- In response to a message of condolence, Irving states, "This is worthy of another Waco Review: much behind the scenes." Irving's friend responds, "Paul, you are so right; this is worthy of another Waco review; my instincts tell me I need to read between the lines!" [560]

Sunday, January 10

- Wyndee Parker, Speaker Pelosi's National Security Advisor, texts Irving, saying, "Pls check you [sic] email. It's tonight's Washington Post article. You are prominently featured." In the records we received, this is the only time she reached out to him via text between August 12th, 2020 and January 10th, 2021. [561]
- Irving texts Chief Sund, saying, "Please call when you're available; just want to sync with press strategy" and "Just read the Post article. Please no worries from me." [562]

Wednesday, January 13

- A friend of Irving's sends him a message of condolence, saying, "You're quite something to take this one for the team, Paul, as they say. I know how these things work and you know I do, too." [563]

APPENDIX

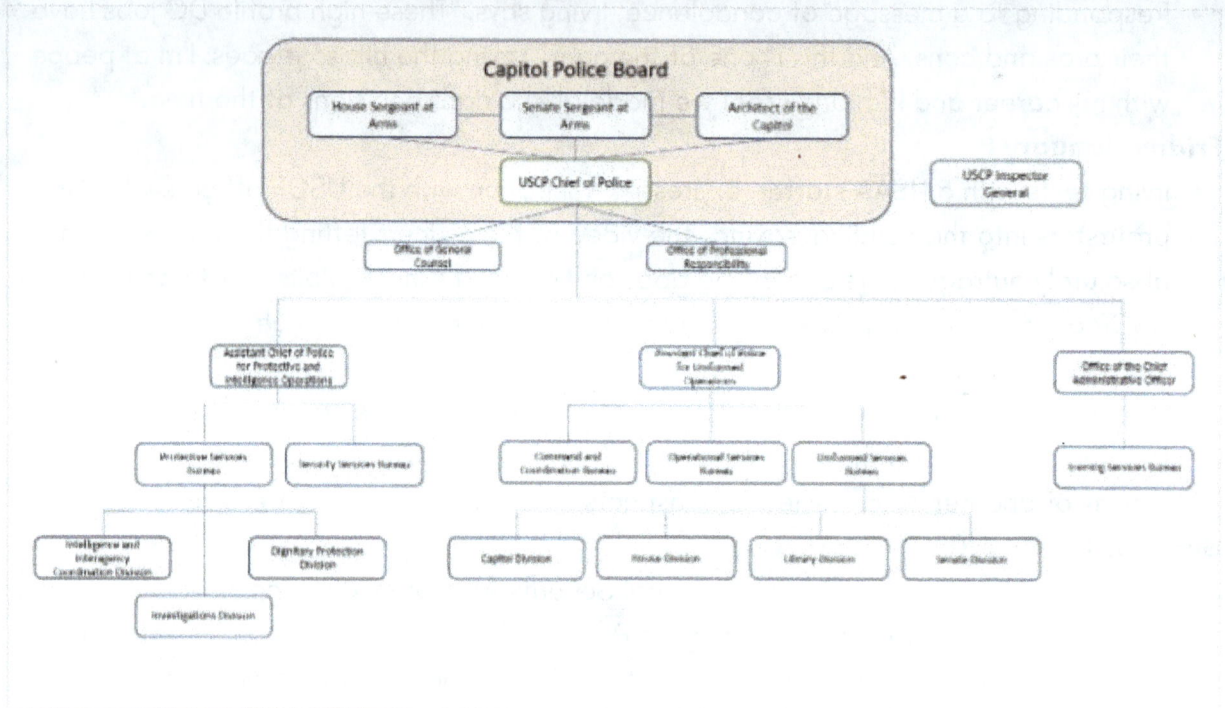

ENDNOTES

1. *See Examining the U.S. Capitol Attack, A Review of the Security, Planning, and Response Failure on January 6*, S. Comm. on Homeland Security and Gov't Affairs & S. Comm on Rules and Administration (June 8, 2021), https://www.hsgac.senate.gov/media/majority-media/peters-portman-klobuchar-blunt-release-bipartisan-report-investigating-january-6th-capitol-attack [hereinafter "Senate Report"].

2. Jenna McLaughlin, *Exclusive: Jan. 6 select committee will include former CIA inspector general found to have retaliated against whistleblower*, Yahoo News (July 23, 2021).

3. 3 U.S.C. §1.

4. 3 U.S.C. §6.

5. *See* Jacqueline Aleman, et al., *Red Flags*, Washington Post (Oct. 31, 2021), www.washingtonpost.com/politics/interactive/2021/warnings-jan-6-insurrection/; see also Transcribed Interview of USCP sources.

6. *See* Jacqueline Aleman, et al., *Red Flags*, Washington Post (Oct. 31, 2021), www.washingtonpost.com/politics/interactive/2021/warnings-jan-6-insurrection/.

7. On December 17, 2020, the FBI shared a memorandum with U.S. Capitol Police that an online post encouraged protesters to shoot police on January 6, 2021. *Red Flags*, Washington Post (Oct. 31, 2021), www.washingtonpost.com/politics/interactive/2021/warnings-jan-6-insurrection/.

8. *Id.*

9. Jacqueline Aleman, et al., *Red Flags*, Washington Post (Oct. 31, 2021), www.washingtonpost.com/politics/interactive/2021/warnings-jan-6-insurrection/.

10. Jacqueline Aleman, et al., *Red Flags*, Washington Post (Oct. 31, 2021), www.washingtonpost.com/politics/interactive/2021/warnings-jan-6-insurrection/.

11. *Id.*

12. Paul Sonne, Peter Hermann and Missy Ryan, *Pentagon placed limits on D.C. Guard ahead of pro-Trump protests due to narrow mission*, Washington Post (Jan. 27, 2021), https://www.washingtonpost.com/national-security/trump-protests-washington-guard-military/2021/01/07/c5299b56-510e-11eb-b2e8-3339e73d9da2_story.html.

13. *Id.*

14. Transcribed Interview of USCP source.

15. Kat Lonsdorf et al, *A timeline of how the Jan. 6 attack unfolded - including who said what and when*, NPR (Jan 5, 2022), https://www.npr.org/2022/01/05/1069977469/a-timeline-of-how-the-jan-6-attack-unfolded-including-who-said-what-and-when.

ENDNOTES

16. Scott Macfarlane & Cassidy McDonald, *January 6 timeline: Key moments from the attack on the Capitol*, CBS News (Jan. 7, 2022), https://www.cbsnews.com/live-updates/january-6-capitol-riot-timeline-key-moments/.

17. *Id.*

18. *Id.*

19. Kat Lonsdorf et al, *A timeline of how the Jan. 6 attack unfolded - including who said what and when*, NPR (Jan. 5, 2022), https://www.npr.org/2022/01/05/1069977469/a-timeline-of-how-the-jan-6-attack-unfolded-including-who-said-what-and-when.

20. Scott Macfarlane & Cassidy McDonald, *January 6 timeline: Key moments from the attack on the Capitol*, CBS News (Jan. 7, 2022), https://www.cbsnews.com/live-updates/january-6-capitol-riot-timeline-key-moments/.

21. *Id.*

22. Kat Lonsdorf et al, *A timeline of how the Jan. 6 attack unfolded - including who said what and when*, NPR (Jan. 5, 2022), https://www.npr.org/2022/01/05/1069977469/a-timeline-of-how-the-jan-6-attack-unfolded-including-who-said-what-and-when.

23. *Id.*

24. *Id.*

25. Scott Macfarlane & Cassidy McDonald, *January 6 timeline: Key moments from the attack on the Capitol*, CBS News (Jan. 7, 2022), https://www.cbsnews.com/live-updates/january-6-capitol-riot-timeline-key-moments/.

26. *Id.*

27. Kayleigh McEnany 45 Archived, @PressSec45, Twitter (Jan. 6, 2021, 3:36 PM).

28. Kat Lonsdorf et al, *A timeline of how the Jan. 6 attack unfolded - including who said what and when*, NPR (Jan. 5, 2022), https://www.npr.org/2022/01/05/1069977469/a-timeline-of-how-the-jan-6-attack-unfolded-including-who-said-what-and-when.

29. *Bill Establishing the United States Capitol Police*, History, Art & Archives, U.S. House of Representatives, https://history.house.gov/HouseRecord/Detail/25769816242?current_search_qs=%3FPreviousSearch%3DSearch%252cAll%252c%252c%252cTitle%26CurrentPage%3D1%26SortOrder%3DTitle%26Command%3DNext.

30. Press Release, S. Comm. on Legislative Branch, H. Comm. on Appropriations, Chair Ryan Statement on U.S. Capitol Police FY 2022 Budget Hearing (Mar. 3, 2021), https://appropriations.house.gov/news/statements/chair-ryan-statement-on-us-capitol-police-fy-2022-budget-hearing.

ENDNOTES

31. Traffic Regulations for the United States Capitol Grounds 238 (amended Feb. 17, 2019), https://www.uscp.gov/sites/uscapitolpolice.house.gov/files/wysiwyg_uploaded/US%20Capitol%20Grounds%20Traffic%20Regulations_Amended%20February%202019.pdf. *The Long Arm of the U.S. Capitol Police by First Branch Forecast was helpful in gathering information for this section.* https://firstbranchforecast.com/2019/08/07/the-long-arm-of-the-u-s-capitol-police/.

32. Stephen W. Stathis & Paul E. Dwyer, Cong. Research Serv., RL30861, Capitol Hill Security: Recent Actions and Organizational Responsibilities (2004),https://www.everycrsreport.com/files/20040203_RL30861_0bb95752db6320d955eec51b7d9895e9cd78c083.pdf.

33. *Id.*

34. Jonathan Allen, Jake Sherman & Molly Ball, *Giffords shooting sparks national debate*, Politico (Jan. 8, 2011),https://www.politico.com/story/2011/01/giffords-shooting-sparks-national-debate-047244.

35. Ewen MacAskill, *US Congress security to be reviewed after Gabrielle Giffords shooting*, The Guardian (Jan. 9, 2011),https://www.theguardian.com/world/2011/jan/09/us-congress-security-review-giffords-shooting.

36. Camila Domonoske, *What We Know About The Suspect In GOP Baseball Practice Shooting*, NPR (June 14, 2017),https://www.npr.org/sections/thetwo-way/2017/06/14/532921612/what-we-know-about-the-suspect-in-gop-baseball-practice-shooting.

37. U.S. Capitol Police, Office of the Inspector General, Review of Intelligence and Interagency Coordination Division Processes and Procedures Surrounding the Protection of Member Events 2022-I-004 3 (May 2022).

38. Chris Marquette, Katherine Tully-McManus & Jennifer Shutt, *Mob fallout: Pelosi calls for Capitol Police chief to be fired; house SAA to resign*, Roll Call (Jan. 7, 2021), https://rollcall.com/2021/01/07/mob-fallout-pelosi-calls-for-capitol-police-chief-to-be-fired-house-saa-to-resign/.

39. Gov't Accountability Office, GAO-17-112, Capitol Police Board: Fully Incorporating Leading Governance Practices Would Help Enhance Accountability, Transparency, and External Communications 13 (2017), https://www.gao.gov/assets/gao-17-112.pdf. [2017 GAO Report]

ENDNOTES

40. Pub. L. No. 117-77, § 3, 135 Stat. 1523.

41. 2017 GAO Report.

42. *Id.* at 5-6.

43. *Id.* at 2.

44. Jennifer Yachnin, *GAO Calls for Overseers' Input on Police Staffing Plan*, Roll Call, July 15, 2003, https://rollcall.com/2003/07/15/gao-calls-for-overseers-input-on-police-staffing-plan/.

45. *Id.*

46. 2017 GAO Report at 8.

47. *Id.* at 8-9.

48. 2017 GAO Report.

49. *Id.* at 14

50. *Id.*

51. *Id.*

52. *Id.*

53. *Id.* at 43.

54. *Id.* at 51.

55. *Reforming The Capitol Police And Improving Accountability For The Capitol Police Board, Hearing before the H. Comm. on House Administration*, 117th Cong. (2021), https://cha.house.gov/committee-activity/hearings/reforming-capitol-police-and-improving-accountability-capitol-police.

56. Gov't Accountability Office, GAO-17-112, Capitol Police Board: Fully Incorporating Leading Governance Practices Would Help Enhance Accountability, Transparency, and External Communications (2017), https://www.gao.gov/assets/gao-17-112.pdf.

57. Press Conference by Nancy Pelosi, Speaker of the House (https://www.c-span.org/video/?517842-1/house-speaker-weekly-briefing)

58. House rule II clause 3(a) and 3(c).

59. *The Latest: Pelosi wants fines for bypassing House security*, AP (Jan. 13, 2021), https://apnews.com/article/donald-trump-politics-adam-kinzinger-liz-cheney-impeachments-2a2431b25720b8815727d4e2fe4e9062.

60. Cristina Marcos, *Pelosi announces lawmakers will be fined $5,000 if they bypass metal detectors to House floor*, The Hill (Jan. 13, 2021), https://thehill.com/homenews/house/534165-pelosi-announces-lawmakers-will-be-fined-if-they-bypass-metal-detectors-to/.

ENDNOTES

61. Claudia Grisales, *Capitol Police are Upping Security Ahead of A Rally In Support Of The Jan. 6 Rioters*, NPR (Sept. 13, 2021), https://www.npr.org/2021/09/13/1036700856/the-u-s-capitol-police-will-reinstall-fencing-ahead-of-a-far-right-rally.

62. *Id.*

63. Rebecca Shabad, *Pelosi tasks retired Lt. Gen. Russel Honore with leading review of Capitol security*, NBC News (Jan. 15, 2021), https://www.nbcnews.com/politics/congress/pelosi-tasks-retired-lt-gen-russel-honor-leading-review-capitol-n1254421.

64. *See* Appendix.

65. *See generally* Texts from documents received by the Committee on House Administration, Minority Staff from House Sergeant at Arms on January 28, 2022.

66. *Id.*

67. *Re: Plans for January 3 and 6*, Email dated December 11, 2020, from documents produced to the Minority Staff of the Committee on House Administration from the House Sergeant at Arms on January 28, 2022.

68. *Id.*

69. *See generally* Emails from documents produced to the Minority Staff of the Committee on House Administration from the House Sergeant at Arms on January 28, 2022.

70. *Id.*

71. *See generally* Emails from documents produced to the Minority Staff of the Committee on House Administration from the House Sergeant at Arms on January 28, 2022.

72. *HOB order*, Emails dated December 15, 2020, from documents produced to the Minority Staff of the Committee on House Administration from the House Sergeant at Arms on January 28, 2022.

73. Text Messages dated December 15, 2020, from documents produced to the Minority Staff of the Committee on House Administration from the House Sergeant at Arms on January 28, 2022.

74. *Id.*

75. *FW: eDC Wednesday January 6 (First Draft)*, Email dated January 3, 2021, from documents produced to the Minority Staff of the Committee on House Administration from the House Sergeant at Arms on January 28, 2022.

76. *Id.*

77. *Id.*

ENDNOTES

78. *See generally* Emails from documents produced to the Minority Staff of the Committee on House Administration from the House Sergeant at Arms on January 28, 2022.

79. *meeting with Chairperson Lofgren*, Email dated January 4, 2021, from documents produced to the Minority Staff of the Committee on House Administration from the House Sergeant at Arms on January 28, 2022.

80. *Id.*

81. Text Message dated January 4, 2021, from documents produced to the Minority Staff of the Committee on House Administration from the House Sergeant at Arms on January 28, 2022.

82. *Draft - Dear Colleague re Security Information for January 6 Joint Session*, Email dated January 4, 2021, from documents produced to the Minority Staff of the Committee on House Administration from the House Sergeant at Arms on January 28, 2022.

83. *RE: Draft - Dear Colleague re Security Information for January 6 Joint Session*, Email dated January 4, 2021, from documents produced to the Minority Staff of the Committee on House Administration from the House Sergeant at Arms on January 28, 2022.

84. *Id.*

85. Text Message dated January 4th, 2021, from documents produced to the Minority Staff of the Committee on House Administration from the House Sergeant at Arms on January 28, 2022.

86. *Id.*

87. *Draft notification*, Email dated January 5, 2021, from documents produced to the Minority Staff of the Committee on House Administration from the House Sergeant at Arms on January 28, 2022.

88. *Id.*

89. *RE: Draft notification*, Email dated January 5, 2021, from documents produced to the Minority Staff of the Committee on House Administration from the House Sergeant at Arms on January 28, 2022.

90. *See generally* Phone records from documents produced to the Minority Staff of the Committee on House Administration from the House Sergeant at Arms on January 28, 2022.

91. *Id.*

92. Mark Mazzetti & Luke Broadwater, *The Lost House: How Confusion and Inaction at the Capitol Delayed a Troop Deployment*, NYT (Feb. 21, 2021), https://www.nytimes.com/2021/02/21/us/politics/capitol-riot-security-delays.html.

93. *Id.*

ENDNOTES

94. *See generally* Phone records from documents produced to the Minority Staff of the Committee on House Administration from the House Sergeant at Arms on January 28, 2022.

95. *Id.*

96. Gov't Accountability Office, GAO-22-105001, Capitol Attack: The Capitol Police Need Clearer Emergency Procedures and a Comprehensive Security Risk Assessment Process 26, (2022).

97. *See* Task Force 1-6, Capitol Security Review (March 5, 2021).

98. Letter from Steve Sund, Former Chief of Police, U.S. Capitol Police, Nancy Pelosi, Speaker, House of Representatives, (Feb. 1, 2021).

99. U.S. Department of Defense, Office of the Inspector General, Review of DOD's Role, Responsibilities, and Actions to Prepare for and Respond to the Protest and Its Aftermath at the U.S. Capitol Campus on January 6, 2021 26 (Nov. 16, 2021).

100. *Id.* at 27.

101. *One follow up question.*, Email dated January 5, 2021, from documents produced to the Minority Staff of the Committee on House Administration from the House Sergeant at Arms on January 28, 2022.

102. Gov't Accountability Office, GAO-22-104829, Capitol Attack: Additional Actions Needed to Better Prepare Capitol Police Officers for Violent Demonstrations 47 (2022).

103. *Id.* at 49.

104. U.S. Capitol Police, Office of the Inspector General, Review of the Events Surrounding the January 6, 2021, Takeover of the U.S. Capitol, Flash Report: Command and Coordination Bureau 13 (July 30, 2021).

105. *Id.*

106. *Id.*

107. Text Messages dated December 9, 2020, from documents produced to the Minority Staff of the Committee on House Administration from the House Sergeant at Arms on January 28, 2022.

108. *Re:* FYI: [Space Redacted] Issue, Email dated December 11, 2020, from documents produced to the Minority Staff of the Committee on House Administration from the House Sergeant at Arms on January 28, 2022.

109. *Id.*

110. *Id.*

111. Text Message dated December 17, 2020, from documents produced to the Minority Staff of the Committee on House Administration from the House Sergeant at Arms on January 28, 2022.

ENDNOTES

112. Text Message dated December 17, 2020, from documents produced to the Minority Staff of the Committee on House Administration from the House Sergeant at Arms on January 28, 2022.

113. *FW: Law Enforcement Partners Meeting*, Email dated December 18, 2020, from documents produced to the Minority Staff of the Committee on House Administration from the House Sergeant at Arms on January 28, 2022.

114. PI Calendar for Tuesday, January 5, 2021, Email dated January 5, 2021, from documents produced to the Minority Staff of the Committee on House Administration from the House Sergeant at Arms on January 28, 2022.

115. Text Messages dated January 5, 2021, from documents produced to the Minority Staff of the Committee on House Administration from the House Sergeant at Arms on January 28, 2022.

116. *Id.*

117. *Id.*

118. Text Message dated January 11, 2021, from documents produced to the Minority Staff of the Committee on House Administration from the House Sergeant at Arms on January 28, 2022.

119. *Tweet by CBS Evening News on Twitter*, Email dated January 5, 2021, from documents produced to the Minority Staff of the Committee on House Administration from the House Sergeant at Arms on January 28, 2022.

120. *CBS reporting re: plane being flown into the Capitol Building tomorrow.*, Email dated January 5, 2021, from documents produced to the Minority Staff of the Committee on House Administration from the House Sergeant at Arms on January 28, 2022.

121. *Re: CBS reporting re: plane being flown into the Capitol Building tomorrow.*, Email dated January 5, 2021, from documents produced to the Minority Staff of the Committee on House Administration from the House Sergeant at Arms on January 28, 2022.

122. *Re: What is going on?*, Email dated January 5, 2021, from documents produced to the Minority Staff of the Committee on House Administration from the House Sergeant at Arms on January 28, 2022.

123. *Id.*

124. *CBS reporting re: plane being flown into the Capitol Building tomorrow.*, Email dated January 5, 2021, from documents produced to the Minority Staff of the Committee on House Administration from the House Sergeant at Arms on January 28, 2022.

ENDNOTES

125. *Fwd: Interest in Tunnels Leading to the US Capitol*, Email dated January 5, 2021, from documents produced to the Minority Staff of the Committee on House Administration from the House Sergeant at Arms on January 28, 2022.

126. *Re: CBS reporting re: plane being flown into the Capitol Building tomorrow.*, Email dated January 5, 2021, from documents produced to the Minority Staff of the Committee on House Administration from the House Sergeant at Arms on January 28, 2022.

127. *Re: CBS reporting re: plane being flown into the Capitol Building tomorrow.*, Email dated January 5, 2021, from documents produced to the Minority Staff of the Committee on House Administration from the House Sergeant at Arms on January 28, 2022.

128. *Fwd: CBS reporting re: plane being flown into the Capitol Building tomorrow.*, Email dated January 5, 2021, from documents produced to the Minority Staff of the Committee on House Administration from the House Sergeant at Arms on January 28, 2022.

129. *Re: CBS reporting re: plane being flown into the Capitol Building tomorrow.*, Email dated January 5, 2021, from documents produced to the Minority Staff of the Committee on House Administration from the House Sergeant at Arms on January 28, 2022.

130. *Id.*

131. Gov't Accountability Office, GAO-22-105001, Capitol Attack: The Capitol Police Need Clearer Emergency Procedures and a Comprehensive Security Risk Assessment Process, 26 (2022).

132. Gov't Accountability Office, GAO-22-105001, Capitol Attack: The Capitol Police Need Clearer Emergency Procedures and a Comprehensive Security Risk Assessment Process, 26 (2022).

133. Transcribed Interview of USCP Chief Tom Manger.

134. Transcribed Interview of USCP Chief Tom Manger.

135. Transcribed Interview of USCP source.

136. Transcribed Interview of USCP source.

137. *See* United States Capitol Police Office of the Inspector General, Review of the Events Surrounding the January 6, 2021, Takeover of the U.S. Capitol, Flash Report: Civil Disturbance Unit and Intelligence, (March 31, 2021).

138. *Id.*

139. *Id.*

140. *Id.*

141. *Id.*

142. Gov't Accountability Office, GAO-22-104829, Capitol Attack: Additional Actions Needed to Better Prepare Capitol Police Officers for Violent Demonstrations, (2022).

ENDNOTES

143. Task Force 1-6, Capitol Security Review 5 (March 5, 2021).

144. Gov't Accountability Office, GAO-22-104829, Capitol Attack: Additional Actions Needed to Better Prepare Capitol Police Officers for Violent Demonstrations, (2022); Task Force 1-6, Capitol Security Review 5 (2021).

145. Transcribed Interview of USCP source.

146. Transcribed Interview of USCP Chief Tom Manger.

147. Transcribed Interview of USCP source.

148. Transcribed Interview of USCP source. (emphasis added)

149. United States Capitol Police Office of the Inspector General, Review of the Events Surrounding the January 6, 2021, Takeover of the U.S. Capitol, Flash Report: Operational Planning and Intelligence, (March 1, 2021).

150. *Id.*

151. *Id.*

152. *Id.*

153. Transcribed Interview of USCP source.

154. United States Capitol Police Office of the Inspector General, Review of the Events Surrounding the January 6, 2021, Takeover of the U.S. Capitol, Flash Report: Civil Disturbance Unit and Intelligence, (March 31, 2021).

155. United States Capitol Police Office of the Inspector General, Review of the Events Surrounding the January 6, 2021, Takeover of the U.S. Capitol, Flash Report: Operational Planning and Intelligence, (March 1, 2021).

156. *Id.*

157. United States Capitol Police Office of the Inspector General, Review of the Events Surrounding the January 6, 2021, Takeover of the U.S. Capitol, Flash Report: Civil Disturbance Unit and Intelligence, (March 31, 2021).

158. *Id.*

159. United States Capitol Police Office of the Inspector General, Review of the Events Surrounding the January 6, 2021, Takeover of the U.S. Capitol, Flash Report: Command and Coordination Bureau, (July 30, 2021).

160. Transcribed Interview of USCP source.

161. Transcribed Interview of USCP source.

162. Transcribed Interview of USCP source.

163. Transcribed Interview of USCP source.

164. Transcribed Interview of USCP source.

165. Transcribed Interview of USCP source.

ENDNOTES

166. Transcribed Interview of USCP source.

167. Transcribed Interview of USCP source.

168. Transcribed Interview of USCP source.

169. Transcribed Interview of USCP source.

170. Transcribed Interview of USCP source.

171. Transcribed Interview of USCP source.

172. Transcribed Interview of USCP source.

173. Transcribed Interview of USCP source.

174. Transcribed Interview of USCP source.

175. Transcribed Interview of USCP source.

176. Transcribed Interview of USCP source.

177. Transcribed Interview of USCP source.

178. Transcribed Interview of USCP source.

179. Transcribed Interview of Julie Farnam.

180. Transcribed Interview of Julie Farnam.

181. Transcribed Interview of Julie Farnam.

182. Transcribed Interview of Julie Farnam.

183. Transcribed Interview of Julie Farnam.

184. Transcribed Interview of USCP source.

185. Transcribed Interview of USCP source.

186. Transcribed Interview of USCP source.

187. Transcribed Interview of Julie Farnam.

188. Transcribed Interview of USCP source.

189. Transcribed Interview of USCP source.

190. Transcribed Interview of Julie Farnam.

191. Transcribed Interview of USCP source.

192. U.S. Capitol Police, Office of the Inspector General, Review of the Events Surrounding the January 6, 2021, Takeover of the U.S. Capitol, Flash Report: Civil Disturbance Unit and Intelligence, 2021-I-003-B 23-24 (March 2021).

193. U.S. Capitol police, Office of the Inspector General, Review of Intelligence and Interagency Coordination Division Processes and Procedures Surrounding the Protection of Member Events 2022-I-004 11-12 (May 2022).

194. Transcribed Interview of Julie Farnam.

195. Transcribed Interview of USCP source.

ENDNOTES

196. Transcribed Interview of Julie Farnam.

197. Transcribed Interview of Julie Farnam.

198. Transcribed Interview of USCP source.

199. Transcribed Interview of USCP source.

200. Transcribed Interview of USCP source.

201. Transcribed Interview of USCP source.

202. Transcribed Interview of USCP source.

203. Transcribed Interview of USCP source.

204. Transcribed Interview of USCP source.

205. Transcribed Interview of USCP source.

206. Transcribed Interview of USCP source.

207. Transcribed Interview of USCP source.

208. Transcribed Interview of USCP source.

209. Transcribed Interview of USCP source.

210. Transcribed Interview of USCP source.

211. Transcribed Interview of USCP source.

212. Transcribed Interview of USCP source.

213. Transcribed Interview of USCP source.

214. Transcribed Interview of USCP source.

215. Transcribed Interview of USCP source.

216. Transcribed Interview of USCP source.

217. Transcribed Interview of Julie Farnam.

218. Intelligence & Interagency Coordination Div., U.S. Capitol Police, Special Event Assessment, 21-A0468 (Dec. 16, 2020).

219. *Id.*

220. Transcribed Interview of USCP source.

221. Transcribed Interview of USCP source.

222. Intelligence & Interagency Coordination Div., U.S. Capitol Police, Investigative Research And Analysis Report, 21-TD-159 (Dec. 21, 2020).

223. *Id.*

224. *See* Senate Report.

225. Senate Report at 41.

226. *Id.* at 40.

227. *Id.* at 41.

228. Transcribed Interview of USCP source.

ENDNOTES

229. Transcribed Interview of USCP source.

230. Transcribed Interview of Julie Farnam.

231. *See* Letter from Anonymous Whistleblower, U.S. Capitol Police, to Nancy P. Pelosi, Speaker, U.S. House of Representatives, Chuck Schumer, Majority Leader, U.S. Senate, Kevin McCarthy, Minority Leader, U.S. House of Representatives, Mitch McConnell, Minority Leader, U.S. Senate (Sept. 28, 2021), https://www.documentcloud.org/documents/21080866-letter#document/p4/a2059186; see also Transcribed Interview of USCP Source.

232. Transcribed Interview of USCP source.

233. Transcribed Interview of USCP source.

234. Intelligence & Interagency Coordination Div., U.S. Capitol Police, Special Event Assessment, 21-A0468 V.3 (Jan. 3, 2021).

235. *Id.*

236. USCP OIG FLASH REPORT 2, at 26.

237. Emails on file with the Committee on House Administration.

238. Emails on file with the Committee on House Administration.

239. Transcribed Interview of Julie Farnam.

240. Transcribed Interview of Julie Farnam.

241. Transcribed Interview of USCP source.

242. Transcribed interview of Julie Farnam.

243. Transcribed interview of Julie Farnam.

244. Transcribed interview of Julie Farnam.

245. Intelligence & Interagency Coordination Div., U.S. Capitol Police, Special Event Assessment 21-A-0468 v.3 (Jan. 3, 2021).

246. Transcribed Interview of Julie Farnam.

247. Transcribed Interview of Julie Farnam.

248. Transcribed Interview of Julie Farnam.

249. *See*, e.g., Grace Segers & Melissa Quinn, How does Congress count electoral votes, and can results be challenged, CBS News (Dec. 23, 2020), https://www.cbsnews.com/news/electoral-college-congress-counts-votes-january-6/.

250. *See* U.S. Const. art. II, sec. 1, cl. 2-3; see also 3 U.S.C. §6.

251. Transcribed Interview of Julie Farnam.

252. Transcribed Interview of Julie Farnam.

253. Transcribed Interview of Julie Farnam.

254. Transcribed Interview of Julie Farnam.

ENDNOTES

255. Transcribed Interview of Julie Farnam.

256. *Examining the U.S. Capitol Attack – Part II: Joint Hearing Before the S. Comm. on Homeland Sec. & Governmental Affairs and the S. Comm. on Rule & Admin., 117th Cong. (2021)* (testimony of Jill Sanborn, Ass't Dir., Counterterrorism Div., Fe. Bureau of Investigation).

257. Transcribed Interview of USCP source.

258. *See* United States Capitol Police Office of the Inspector General, Review of the Events Surrounding the January 6, 2021, Takeover of the U.S. Capitol, Flash Report: Command and Coordination Bureau, (July 30, 2021).

259. Transcribed Interview of USCP source.

260. Transcribed Interview of USCP Chief Tom Manger.

261. Transcribed Interview of USCP source.

262. Transcribed Interview of USCP Chief Tom Manger.

263. Transcribed Interview of USCP Chief Tom Manger.

264. Transcribed Interview of William Walker.

265. Transcribed Interview of William Walker.

266. Betsy Woodruff Swan & Daniel Lippman, *Capitol Police examines backgrounds, social media feeds of some who meet with lawmakers*, Politico (Jan. 24, 2022) https://www.politico.com/news/2022/01/24/capitol-police-social-media-00000948.

267. Transcribed Interview of USCP source.

268. Betsy Woodruff Swan & Daniel Lippman, *Capitol Police examines backgrounds, social media feeds of some who meet with lawmakers*, Politico (Jan. 24, 2022) https://www.politico.com/news/2022/01/24/capitol-police-social-media-00000948.

269. Letter from House Republicans to the Capitol Police Board (Jan. 25, 2022).

270. Letter from J. Thomas Manger, Chief of Police, U.S. Capitol Police, to House Republicans (Jan. 27, 2022).

271. *See* United States Capitol Police Office of the Inspector General, Review of Intelligence and Interagency Coordination Division Processes and Procedures Surrounding the Protection of Member Events (May 10, 2022).

272. Transcribed Interview of USCP source.

273. Transcribed Interview of USCP source. (emphasis added)

274. Transcribed Interview of USCP Chief Tom Manger.

275. Transcribed Interview of USCP Chief Tom Manger.

276. January 6, 2021 Event, After-Action Report, U.S. Capitol Police (June 4, 2021).

ENDNOTES

277. Note: this is an important step toward encouraging confidence from the Board and USCP.

278. *Intelligence and Interagency Coordination Division Daily Intelligence Report Thursday, December 3, 2020*, Email dated December 3, 2020, from documents produced to the Minority Staff of the Committee on House Administration from the House Sergeant at Arms on January 28, 2022.

279. *Office of the Sergeant at Arms With United States Capitol Police Daily Intelligence Brief Thursday, December 3, 2020*, Email dated December 3, 2020, from documents produced to the Minority Staff of the Committee on House Administration from the House Sergeant at Arms on January 28, 2022.

280. Text Message dated December 5, 2020, from documents produced to the Minority Staff of the Committee on House Administration from the House Sergeant at Arms on January 28, 2022.

281. Text Message dated December 6, 2020, from documents produced to the Minority Staff of the Committee on House Administration from the House Sergeant at Arms on January 28, 2022.

282. Text Message dated December 8, 2020, from documents produced to the Minority Staff of the Committee on House Administration from the House Sergeant at Arms on January 28, 2022.

283. Text Message dated December 9, 2020, from documents produced to the Minority Staff of the Committee on House Administration from the House Sergeant at Arms on January 28, 2022.

284. Text Message dated December 9, 2020, from documents produced to the Minority Staff of the Committee on House Administration from the House Sergeant at Arms on January 28, 2022.

285. *Re: FYI: [Space Redacted] Issue*, Email dated December 11, 2020, from documents produced to the Minority Staff of the Committee on House Administration from the House Sergeant at Arms on January 28, 2022.

286. *Re: Plans for January 3 and 6*, Email dated December 11, 2020, from documents produced to the Minority Staff of the Committee on House Administration from the House Sergeant at Arms on January 28, 2022.

287. Text Message dated December 14, 2020, from documents produced to the Minority Staff of the Committee on House Administration from the House Sergeant at Arms on January 28, 2022.

ENDNOTES

288. *PI Calendar for Tuesday, December 15, 2020*, Email dated December 15, 2020, from documents produced to the Minority Staff of the Committee on House Administration from the House Sergeant at Arms on January 28, 2022.

289. *HOB order*, Email dated December 15, 2020, from documents produced to the Minority Staff of the Committee on House Administration from the House Sergeant at Arms on January 28, 2022.

290. Text Message dated December 15, 2020, from documents produced to the Minority Staff of the Committee on House Administration from the House Sergeant at Arms on January 28, 2022.

291. *Intelligence and Interagency Coordination Division Daily Intelligence Report Friday December 16, 2020*, Email dated December 16, 2020, from documents produced to the Minority Staff of the Committee on House Administration from the House Sergeant at Arms on January 28, 2022.

292. *Office of the Sergeant at Arms With United States Capitol Police Daily Intelligence Brief Wednesday, December 16, 2020*, Email dated December 16, 2020, from documents produced to the Minority Staff of the Committee on House Administration from the House Sergeant at Arms on January 28, 2022.

293. Text Message dated December 16, 2020, from documents produced to the Minority Staff of the Committee on House Administration from the House Sergeant at Arms on January 28, 2022.

294. Text Message dated December 17, 2020, from documents produced to the Minority Staff of the Committee on House Administration from the House Sergeant at Arms on January 28, 2022.

295. *FW: Law Enforcement Partners Meeting*, Email dated December 18, 2020, from documents produced to the Minority Staff of the Committee on House Administration from the House Sergeant at Arms on January 28, 2022.

296. Text Message dated December 18, 2020, from documents produced to the Minority Staff of the Committee on House Administration from the House Sergeant at Arms on January 28, 2022.

297. Text Message dated December 20, 2020, from documents produced to the Minority Staff of the Committee on House Administration from the House Sergeant at Arms on January 28, 2022.

298. *Office of the Sergeant at Arms With United States Capitol Police Daily Intelligence Brief Monday, December 21, 2020*, Email dated December 21, 2020, from documents produced to the Minority Staff of the Committee on House Administration from the House Sergeant at Arms on January 28, 2022.

ENDNOTES

299. *Office of the Sergeant at Arms With United States Capitol Police Daily Intelligence Brief Monday, December 28, 2020*, Email dated December 28, 2020, from documents produced to the Minority Staff of the Committee on House Administration from the House Sergeant at Arms on January 28, 2022.

300. Text Message dated December 29, 2020, from documents produced to the Minority Staff of the Committee on House Administration from the House Sergeant at Arms on January 28, 2022.

301. FW: Draft – Immediate Office staff schedule for January, Email dated December 29, 2020, from documents produced to the Minority Staff of the Committee on House Administration from the House Sergeant at Arms on January 28, 2022.

302. *Office of the Sergeant at Arms With United States Capitol Police Daily Intelligence Brief Wednesday, December 30, 2020*, Email dated December 30, 2020, from documents produced to the Minority Staff of the Committee on House Administration from the House Sergeant at Arms on January 28, 2022.

303. *Office of the Sergeant at Arms With United States Capitol Police Daily Intelligence Brief Report Thursday, December 31, 2020*, Email dated December 31, 2020, from documents produced to the Minority Staff of the Committee on House Administration from the House Sergeant at Arms on January 28, 2022.

304. Text Message dated January 2, 2021, from documents produced to the Minority Staff of the Committee on House Administration from the House Sergeant at Arms on January 28, 2022.

305. *Accepted: Intel brief for Wednesday*, Email dated January 3, 2021, from documents produced to the Minority Staff of the Committee on House Administration from the House Sergeant at Arms on January 28, 2022.

306. *FW: eDC Wednesday January 6 (First Draft)*, Email dated January 3, 2021, from documents produced to the Minority Staff of the Committee on House Administration from the House Sergeant at Arms on January 28, 2022.

307. Text Message dated January 3, 2021, from documents produced to the Minority Staff of the Committee on House Administration from the House Sergeant at Arms on January 28, 2022.

308. Text Message dated January 4, 2021, from documents produced to the Minority Staff of the Committee on House Administration from the House Sergeant at Arms on January 28, 2022.

ENDNOTES

309. *meeting [sic] with Chairperson Lofgren*, Email dated January 4, 2021, from documents produced to the Minority Staff of the Committee on House Administration from the House Sergeant at Arms on January 28, 2022.

310. Text Message dated January 4, 2021, from documents produced to the Minority Staff of the Committee on House Administration from the House Sergeant at Arms on January 28, 2022.

311. *FW: Updated Assessment*, Email dated January 4, 2021, from documents produced to the Minority Staff of the Committee on House Administration from the House Sergeant at Arms on January 28, 2022.

312. Office of the Sergeant at Arms With United States Capitol Police Daily Intelligence Brief Monday, January 4, 2021, Email dated January 4, 2021, from documents produced to the Minority Staff of the Committee on House Administration from the House Sergeant at Arms on January 28, 2022.

313. Accepted: Meet in Paul's office to do Electoral college call with Speaker's team, Email dated January 3, 2021, from documents produced to the Minority Staff of the Committee on House Administration from the House Sergeant at Arms on January 28, 2022.

314. *Draft - Dear Colleague re Security Information for January 6 Joint Session*, Email dated January 4, 2021, from documents produced to the Minority Staff of the Committee on House Administration from the House Sergeant at Arms on January 28, 2022.

315. *RE: Draft - Dear Colleague re Security Information for January 6 Joint Session*, Email dated January 4, 2021, from documents produced to the Minority Staff of the Committee on House Administration from the House Sergeant at Arms on January 28, 2022.

316. *RE: Draft - Dear Colleague re Security Information for January 6 Joint Session*, Email dated January 4, 2021, from documents produced to the Minority Staff of the Committee on House Administration from the House Sergeant at Arms on January 28, 2022.

317. *RE: Draft - Dear Colleague re Security Information for January 6 Joint Session*, Email dated January 4, 2021, from documents produced to the Minority Staff of the Committee on House Administration from the House Sergeant at Arms on January 28, 2022.

318. Text Message dated January 4, 2021, from documents produced to the Minority Staff of the Committee on House Administration from the House Sergeant at Arms on January 28, 2022.

319. *Security Information - Wednesday, January 6 Joint Session*, Email dated January 4, 2021, from the Office of the Sergeant at Arms.

ENDNOTES

320. *TAS Criminal Threat Notification – [Senator's name redacted] 01.04.2021 – #2*, Email dated January 4, 2021, from documents produced to the Minority Staff of the Committee on House Administration from the House Sergeant at Arms on January 28, 2022.

321. Text Message dated January 4, 2021, from documents produced to the Minority Staff of the Committee on House Administration from the House Sergeant at Arms on January 28, 2022.

322. *RE: Draft timeline*, Email dated January 5, 2021, from documents produced to the Minority Staff of the Committee on House Administration from the House Sergeant at Arms on January 28, 2022.

323. *PI Calendar for Tuesday, January 5, 2021*, Email dated January 5, 2021, from documents produced to the Minority Staff of the Committee on House Administration from the House Sergeant at Arms on January 28, 2022.

324. *Walkthrough for Electoral College Joint Session*, Email dated January 5, 2021, from documents produced to the Minority Staff of the Committee on House Administration from the House Sergeant at Arms on January 28, 2022.

325. *Draft notification*, Email dated January 5, 2021, from documents produced to the Minority Staff of the Committee on House Administration from the House Sergeant at Arms on January 28, 2022.

326. *PI Calendar for Tuesday, January 5, 2021*, Email dated January 5, 2021, from documents produced to the Minority Staff of the Committee on House Administration from the House Sergeant at Arms on January 28, 2022.

327. *Intelligence and Interagency Coordination Division Daily Intelligence Report Tuesday, January 5, 2021*, Email dated January 5, 2021, from documents produced to the Minority Staff of the Committee on House Administration from the House Sergeant at Arms on January 28, 2022.

328. *RE: Draft Electoral College notification [sic]*, Email dated January 5, 2021, from documents produced to the Minority Staff of the Committee on House Administration from the House Sergeant at Arms on January 28, 2022.

329. *TAS Criminal Threat Notification – [Senator's name redacted] 01.05.2021*, Email dated January 5, 2021, from documents produced to the Minority Staff of the Committee on House Administration from the House Sergeant at Arms on January 28, 2022.

330. *Ready for Tomorrow*, Email dated January 5, 2021, from documents produced to the Minority Staff of the Committee on House Administration from the House Sergeant at Arms on January 28, 2022.

ENDNOTES

331. *RE: Draft notification*, Email dated January 5, 2021, from documents produced to the Minority Staff of the Committee on House Administration from the House Sergeant at Arms on January 28, 2022.

332. *PI Calendar for Tuesday, January 5, 2021*, Email dated January 5, 2021, from documents produced to the Minority Staff of the Committee on House Administration from the House Sergeant at Arms on January 28, 2022.

333. *Dear Colleague Follow Up*, Email dated January 5, 2021, from documents produced to the Minority Staff of the Committee on House Administration from the House Sergeant at Arms on January 28, 2022.

334. *RE: Draft notification*, Email dated January 5, 2021, from documents produced to the Minority Staff of the Committee on House Administration from the House Sergeant at Arms on January 28, 2022.

335. *RE: Dear Colleague Follow Up*, Email dated January 5, 2021, from documents produced to the Minority Staff of the Committee on House Administration from the House Sergeant at Arms on January 28, 2022.

336. *This has both of Terri's requests in it*, Email dated January 5, 2021, from documents produced to the Minority Staff of the Committee on House Administration from the House Sergeant at Arms on January 28, 2022.

337. *RE: Dear Colleague Follow Up*, Email dated January 5, 2021, from documents produced to the Minority Staff of the Committee on House Administration from the House Sergeant at Arms on January 28, 2022.

338. *latest version*, Email dated January 5, 2021, from documents produced to the Minority Staff of the Committee on House Administration from the House Sergeant at Arms on January 28, 2022.

339. *Electoral College W/T*, Email dated January 5, 2021, from documents produced to the Minority Staff of the Committee on House Administration from the House Sergeant at Arms on January 28, 2022.

340. *Masks on floor*, Email dated January 5, 2021, from documents produced to the Minority Staff of the Committee on House Administration from the House Sergeant at Arms on January 28, 2022.

341. *FW: meeting with Paul today*, Email dated January 5, 2021, from documents produced to the Minority Staff of the Committee on House Administration from the House Sergeant at Arms on January 28, 2022.

ENDNOTES

342. *2021_01_06_Electoral College_v3*, Email dated January 5, 2021, from documents produced to the Minority Staff of the Committee on House Administration from the House Sergeant at Arms on January 28, 2022.

343. *2021_01_05_21_First Amendment Activities Follow Up.pdf*, Email dated January 5, 2021, from documents produced to the Minority Staff of the Committee on House Administration from the House Sergeant at Arms on January 28, 2022.

344. *RE: 2021_01_05_21_First Amendment Activities Follow Up.pdf*, Email dated January 5, 2021, from documents produced to the Minority Staff of the Committee on House Administration from the House Sergeant at Arms on January 28, 2022.

345. *Dear Colleague - Wednesday January 6 Road Closures*, Email dated January 5, 2021, from documents produced to the Minority Staff of the Committee on House Administration from the House Sergeant at Arms on January 28, 2022.

346. *Accepted: Meet re evac plan for tomorrow - Tim, Fitz, Erik*, Email dated January 5, 2021, from documents produced to the Minority Staff of the Committee on House Administration from the House Sergeant at Arms on January 28, 2022.

347. *FW: Bike rack for January 6*, Email dated January 5, 2021, from documents produced to the Minority Staff of the Committee on House Administration from the House Sergeant at Arms on January 28, 2022.

348. *Perimeter*, Email dated January 5, 2021, from documents produced to the Minority Staff of the Committee on House Administration from the House Sergeant at Arms on January 28, 2022.

349. *FW: Perimeter*, Email dated January 5, 2021, from documents produced to the Minority Staff of the Committee on House Administration from the House Sergeant at Arms on January 28, 2022.

350. *Accepted: Brief Chairman Ryan on threats*, Email dated January 5, 2021, from documents produced to the Minority Staff of the Committee on House Administration from the House Sergeant at Arms on January 28, 2022.

351. *Dear Colleague: Joint Session to Count Electoral Votes*, Email from the Office of the Sergeant at Arms, dated January 5, 2021.

352. Text Message dated January 5, 2021, from documents produced to the Minority Staff of the Committee on House Administration from the House Sergeant at Arms on January 28, 2022.

353. Text Message dated January 5, 2021, from documents produced to the Minority Staff of the Committee on House Administration from the House Sergeant at Arms on January 28, 2022.

ENDNOTES

354. *Dear Colleague: Road Closures - Wednesday, January 6 Joint Session*, Email from the Office of the Sergeant at Arms, dated January 5, 2021.

355. *One follow up question.*, Email dated January 5, 2021, from documents produced to the Minority Staff of the Committee on House Administration from the House Sergeant at Arms on January 28, 2022.

356. *Re: One follow up question.*, Email dated January 5, 2021, from documents produced to the Minority Staff of the Committee on House Administration from the House Sergeant at Arms on January 28, 2022.

357. Text Message dated January 5, 2021, from documents produced to the Minority Staff of the Committee on House Administration from the House Sergeant at Arms on January 28, 2022.

358. *Re:6:30*, Email dated January 5, 2021, from documents produced to the Minority Staff of the Committee on House Administration from the House Sergeant at Arms on January 28, 2022.

359. *Re:6:30*, Email dated January 5, 2021, from documents produced to the Minority Staff of the Committee on House Administration from the House Sergeant at Arms on January 28, 2022.

360. Text Message dated January 5, 2021, from documents produced to the Minority Staff of the Committee on House Administration from the House Sergeant at Arms on January 28, 2022.

361. *Re: 6:30*, Email dated January 5, 2021, from documents produced to the Minority Staff of the Committee on House Administration from the House Sergeant at Arms on January 28, 2022.

326. Tweet by CBS Evening News on Twitter, Email dated January 5, 2021, from documents produced to the Minority Staff of the Committee on House Administration from the House Sergeant at Arms on January 28, 2022.

363. *CBS reporting re: plane being flown into the Capitol Building tomorrow.*, Email dated January 5, 2021, from documents produced to the Minority Staff of the Committee on House Administration from the House Sergeant at Arms on January 28, 2022.

364. *Re: CBS reporting re: plane being flown into the Capitol Building tomorrow.*, Email dated January 5, 2021, from documents produced to the Minority Staff of the Committee on House Administration from the House Sergeant at Arms on January 28, 2022.

365. *Re: What is going on?*, Email dated January 5, 2021, from documents produced to the Minority Staff of the Committee on House Administration from the House Sergeant at Arms on January 28, 2022.

ENDNOTES

366. *Re: CBS reporting re: plane being flown into the Capitol Building tomorrow.*, Email dated January 5, 2021, from documents produced to the Minority Staff of the Committee on House Administration from the House Sergeant at Arms on January 28, 2022.

367. *Fwd: Interest in Tunnels Leading to the US Capitol*, Email dated January 5, 2021, from documents produced to the Minority Staff of the Committee on House Administration from the House Sergeant at Arms on January 28, 2022.

368. *Fwd: CBS reporting re: plane being flown into the Capitol Building tomorrow.*, Email dated January 5, 2021, from documents produced to the Minority Staff of the Committee on House Administration from the House Sergeant at Arms on January 28, 2022.

369. *Re: //CUI/LES//Changes to the Security Perimeter*, Email dated January 5, 2021, from documents produced to the Minority Staff of the Committee on House Administration from the Architect of the Capitol on April 20, 2021.

370. *Re: CBS reporting re: plane being flown into the Capitol Building tomorrow.*, Email dated January 5, 2021, from documents produced to the Minority Staff of the Committee on House Administration from the House Sergeant at Arms on January 28, 2022.

371. *Fwd: CBS reporting re: plane being flown into the Capitol Building tomorrow.*, Email dated January 5, 2021, from documents produced to the Minority Staff of the Committee on House Administration from the House Sergeant at Arms on January 28, 2022.

372. *Re: CBS reporting re: plane being flown into the Capitol Building tomorrow.*, Email dated January 5, 2021, from documents produced to the Minority Staff of the Committee on House Administration from the House Sergeant at Arms on January 28, 2022.

373. *Re: CBS reporting re: plane being flown into the Capitol Building tomorrow.*, Email dated January 5, 2021, from documents produced to the Minority Staff of the Committee on House Administration from the House Sergeant at Arms on January 28, 2022.

374. *Re: CBS reporting re: plane being flown into the Capitol Building tomorrow.*, Email dated January 5, 2021, from documents produced to the Minority Staff of the Committee on House Administration from the House Sergeant at Arms on January 28, 2022.

375. *Re: //CUI/LES//Changes to the Security Perimeter*, Email dated January 5, 2021, from documents produced to the Minority Staff of the Committee on House Administration from the Architect of the Capitol on April 20, 2021.

376. *COVID positive*, Email dated January 5, 2021, from documents produced to the Minority Staff of the Committee on House Administration from the House Sergeant at Arms on January 28, 2022.

ENDNOTES

377. *Re: CBS reporting re: plane being flown into the Capitol Building tomorrow.*, Email dated January 5, 2021, from documents produced to the Minority Staff of the Committee on House Administration from the House Sergeant at Arms on January 28, 2022.

378. *SCIF*, Email dated January 5, 2021, from documents produced to the Minority Staff of the Committee on House Administration from the House Sergeant at Arms on January 28, 2022.

379. Text Message dated January 6, 2021, from documents produced to the Minority Staff of the Committee on House Administration from the House Sergeant at Arms on January 28, 2022.

380. Phone records from documents produced to the Minority Staff of the Committee on House Administration from the House Sergeant at Arms on January 28, 2022.

381. *Numbers on Floor today (January 6, 2021)*, Email dated January 6, 2021, from documents produced to the Minority Staff of the Committee on House Administration from the House Sergeant at Arms on January 28, 2022.

382. *FW: Demos/Map – Wed, 1/6/2021*, Email dated January 6, 2021, from documents produced to the Minority Staff of the Committee on House Administration from the House Sergeant at Arms on January 28, 2022.

383. *Re: //CUI/LES//Changes to the Security Perimeter*, Email dated January 6, 2021, from documents produced to the Minority Staff of the Committee on House Administration from the Architect of the Capitol on April 20, 2021.

384. *FW: 01/06/2021 – Planned Demonstrations in Washington, DC Update #1*, Email dated January 6, 2021, from documents produced to the Minority Staff of the Committee on House Administration from the House Sergeant at Arms on January 28, 2022.

385. *Thinking of you today*, Email dated January 6, 2021, from documents produced to the Minority Staff of the Committee on House Administration from the House Sergeant at Arms on January 28, 2022.

386. Phone records from documents produced to the Minority Staff of the Committee on House Administration from the House Sergeant at Arms on January 28, 2022.

387. *Police Response – N CVC Walkway*, Email dated January 6, 2021, from documents produced to the Minority Staff of the Committee on House Administration from the House Sergeant at Arms on January 28, 2022.

388. *Police Response – N CVC Walkway (final)*, Email dated January 6, 2021, from documents produced to the Minority Staff of the Committee on House Administration from the House Sergeant at Arms on January 28, 2022.

ENDNOTES

389. *Issue exposed*, Email dated January 6, 2021, from documents produced to the Minority Staff of the Committee on House Administration from the House Sergeant at Arms on January 28, 2022.

390. *RE: Issue exposed*, Email dated January 6, 2021, from documents produced to the Minority Staff of the Committee on House Administration from the House Sergeant at Arms on January 28, 2022.

391. *RE: Issue exposed*, Email dated January 6, 2021, from documents produced to the Minority Staff of the Committee on House Administration from the House Sergeant at Arms on January 28, 2022.

392. Phone records from documents produced to the Minority Staff of the Committee on House Administration from the House Sergeant at Arms on January 28, 2022.

393. Text Message dated January 6, 2021, from documents produced to the Minority Staff of the Committee on House Administration from the House Sergeant at Arms on January 28, 2022.

394. Phone records from documents produced to the Minority Staff of the Committee on House Administration from the House Sergeant at Arms on January 28, 2022.

395. *Suggested language for note card we discussed*, Email dated January 6, 2021, from documents produced to the Minority Staff of the Committee on House Administration from the House Sergeant at Arms on January 28, 2022.

396. *FSA: BOLO for suspicious-looking truck*, Email dated January 6, 2021, from documents produced to the Minority Staff of the Committee on House Administration from the House Sergeant at Arms on January 28, 2022.

397. Phone records from documents produced to the Minority Staff of the Committee on House Administration from the House Sergeant at Arms on January 28, 2022.

398. *RE: Suggested language for note card we discussed*, Email dated January 6, 2021, from documents produced to the Minority Staff of the Committee on House Administration from the House Sergeant at Arms on January 28, 2022.

399. *Fwd: Suggested language for note card we discussed*, Email dated January 6, 2021, from documents produced to the Minority Staff of the Committee on House Administration from the House Sergeant at Arms on January 28, 2022.

400. *RE: Suggested language for note card we discussed*, Email dated January 6, 2021, from documents produced to the Minority Staff of the Committee on House Administration from the House Sergeant at Arms on January 28, 2022.

ENDNOTES

401. *Office of the Sergeant at Arms With United States Capitol Police Daily Intelligence Brief Wednesday, January 6, 2021*, Email dated January 6, 2021, from documents produced to the Minority Staff of the Committee on House Administration from the House Sergeant at Arms on January 28, 2022.

402. *Demonstration Activity - eastbound on the Mall toward Capitol*, Email dated January 6, 2021, from documents produced to the Minority Staff of the Committee on House Administration from the House Sergeant at Arms on January 28, 2022.

403. *Fwd: Update #1*, Email dated January 6, 2021, from documents produced to the Minority Staff of the Committee on House Administration from the House Sergeant at Arms on January 28, 2022.

404. *Fwd: Suggested language for note card we discussed*, Email dated January 6, 2021, from documents produced to the Minority Staff of the Committee on House Administration from the House Sergeant at Arms on January 28, 2022.

405. *Re: Suggested language for note card we discussed*, Email dated January 6, 2021, from documents produced to the Minority Staff of the Committee on House Administration from the House Sergeant at Arms on January 28, 2022.

406. *Demonstration Activity - Proud Boys*, Email dated January 6, 2021, from documents produced to the Minority Staff of the Committee on House Administration from the House Sergeant at Arms on January 28, 2022.

407. *Re: Suggested language for note card we discussed*, Email dated January 6, 2021, from documents produced to the Minority Staff of the Committee on House Administration from the House Sergeant at Arms on January 28, 2022.

408. *USCP Response - Senate Egg*, Email dated January 6, 2021, from documents produced to the Minority Staff of the Committee on House Administration from the House Sergeant at Arms on January 28, 2022.

409. *Demonstration Activity - Proud Boys (update 2)*, Email dated January 6, 2021, from documents produced to the Minority Staff of the Committee on House Administration from the House Sergeant at Arms on January 28, 2022.

410. *Re: Suggested language for note card we discussed*, Email dated January 6, 2021, from documents produced to the Minority Staff of the Committee on House Administration from the House Sergeant at Arms on January 28, 2022.

411. *Demonstration Activity - Proud Boys (update 3)*, Email dated January 6, 2021, from documents produced to the Minority Staff of the Committee on House Administration from the House Sergeant at Arms on January 28, 2022.

ENDNOTES

412. *Demonstration Activity - Proud Boys (update 4)*, Email dated January 6, 2021, from documents produced to the Minority Staff of the Committee on House Administration from the House Sergeant at Arms on January 28, 2022.

413. Phone records from documents produced to the Minority Staff of the Committee on House Administration from the House Sergeant at Arms on January 28, 2022.

414. *RE: Suggested language for note card we discussed*, Email dated January 6, 2021, from documents produced to the Minority Staff of the Committee on House Administration from the House Sergeant at Arms on January 28, 2022.

415. *Fwd: Quarantine order*, Email dated January 6, 2021, from documents produced to the Minority Staff of the Committee on House Administration from the House Sergeant at Arms on January 28, 2022.

416. *Police Activity - 2nd and Con NW*, Email dated January 6, 2021, from documents produced to the Minority Staff of the Committee on House Administration from the House Sergeant at Arms on January 28, 2022.

417. *Fwd: Quarantine order*, Email dated January 6, 2021, from documents produced to the Minority Staff of the Committee on House Administration from the House Sergeant at Arms on January 28, 2022.

418. *FW: Document1*, Email dated January 6, 2021, from documents produced to the Minority Staff of the Committee on House Administration from the House Sergeant at Arms on January 28, 2022.

419. *FW: Trump says he's coming to Capitol Hill*, Email dated January 6, 2021, from documents produced to the Minority Staff of the Committee on House Administration from the House Sergeant at Arms on January 28, 2022.

420. *FW: Trump says he's coming to Capitol Hill*, Email dated January 6, 2021, from documents produced to the Minority Staff of the Committee on House Administration from the House Sergeant at Arms on January 28, 2022.

421. *RE: Trump says he's coming to Capitol Hill*, Email dated January 6, 2021, from documents produced to the Minority Staff of the Committee on House Administration from the House Sergeant at Arms on January 28, 2022.

422. *Crowd estimates*, Email dated January 6, 2021, from documents produced to the Minority Staff of the Committee on House Administration from the House Sergeant at Arms on January 28, 2022.

423. *RE: Crowd estimates*, Email dated January 6, 2021, from documents produced to the Minority Staff of the Committee on House Administration from the House Sergeant at Arms on January 28, 2022.

ENDNOTES

424. Phone records from documents produced to the Minority Staff of the Committee on House Administration from the House Sergeant at Arms on January 28, 2022.

425. *Demonstration Update (update 2)*, Email dated January 6, 2021, from documents produced to the Minority Staff of the Committee on House Administration from the House Sergeant at Arms on January 28, 2022.

426. Phone records from documents produced to the Minority Staff of the Committee on House Administration from the House Sergeant at Arms on January 28, 2022.

427. *Demonstration Update (update 3)*, Email dated January 6, 2021, from documents produced to the Minority Staff of the Committee on House Administration from the House Sergeant at Arms on January 28, 2022.

428. *March to US Capitol*, Email dated January 6, 2021, from documents produced to the Minority Staff of the Committee on House Administration from the House Sergeant at Arms on January 28, 2022.

429. Phone records from documents produced to the Minority Staff of the Committee on House Administration from the House Sergeant at Arms on January 28, 2022.

430. *Possible [redacted] – RNC*, Email dated January 6, 2021, from documents produced to the Minority Staff of the Committee on House Administration from the House Sergeant at Arms on January 28, 2022.

431. *Priority – Breach on West Front*, Email dated January 6, 2021, from documents produced to the Minority Staff of the Committee on House Administration from the House Sergeant at Arms on January 28, 2022.

432. Phone records from documents produced to the Minority Staff of the Committee on House Administration from the House Sergeant at Arms on January 28, 2022.

433. Text Message dated January 6, 2021, from documents produced to the Minority Staff of the Committee on House Administration from the House Sergeant at Arms on January 28, 2022.

434. *Priority – Breach on West Front*, Email dated January 6, 2021, from documents produced to the Minority Staff of the Committee on House Administration from the House Sergeant at Arms on January 28, 2022.

435. *Building Evacuation – Madison*, Email dated January 6, 2021, from documents produced to the Minority Staff of the Committee on House Administration from the House Sergeant at Arms on January 28, 2022.

436. *West front*, Email dated January 6, 2021, from documents produced to the Minority Staff of the Committee on House Administration from the House Sergeant at Arms on January 28, 2022.

ENDNOTES

437. *[redacted] DNC*, Email dated January 6, 2021, from documents produced to the Minority Staff of the Committee on House Administration from the House Sergeant at Arms on January 28, 2022.

438. *Building Evacuation: CANNON*, Email dated January 6, 2021, from documents produced to the Minority Staff of the Committee on House Administration from the House Sergeant at Arms on January 28, 2022.

439. *FW: 01/06/2021 - Planned Demonstrations in Washington, DC Update #14*, Email dated January 6, 2021, from documents produced to the Minority Staff of the Committee on House Administration from the House Sergeant at Arms on January 28, 2022.

440. *Re: Crowd estimates*, Email dated January 6, 2021, from documents produced to the Minority Staff of the Committee on House Administration from the House Sergeant at Arms on January 28, 2022.

441. *Priority - Breach on West Front (update)*, Email dated January 6, 2021, from documents produced to the Minority Staff of the Committee on House Administration from the House Sergeant at Arms on January 28, 2022.

442. *RE: Crowd estimates*, Email dated January 6, 2021, from documents produced to the Minority Staff of the Committee on House Administration from the House Sergeant at Arms on January 28, 2022.

443. *Re: Crowd estimates*, Email dated January 6, 2021, from documents produced to the Minority Staff of the Committee on House Administration from the House Sergeant at Arms on January 28, 2022.

444. Phone records from documents produced to the Minority Staff of the Committee on House Administration from the House Sergeant at Arms on January 28, 2022.

445. Phone records from documents produced to the Minority Staff of the Committee on House Administration from the House Sergeant at Arms on January 28, 2022.

446. Phone records from documents produced to the Minority Staff of the Committee on House Administration from the House Sergeant at Arms on January 28, 2022.

447. Text Message dated January 6, 2021, from documents produced to the Minority Staff of the Committee on House Administration from the House Sergeant at Arms on January 28, 2022.

448. Phone records from documents produced to the Minority Staff of the Committee on House Administration from the House Sergeant at Arms on January 28, 2022.

449. *Priority - Breach on West Front (update)*, Email dated January 6, 2021, from documents produced to the Minority Staff of the Committee on House Administration from the House Sergeant at Arms on January 28, 2022.

ENDNOTES

450. Phone records from documents produced to the Minority Staff of the Committee on House Administration from the House Sergeant at Arms on January 28, 2022.

451. *Priority – Breach on West Front (update)*, Email dated January 6, 2021, from documents produced to the Minority Staff of the Committee on House Administration from the House Sergeant at Arms on January 28, 2022.

452. *RE: Crowd estimates*, Email dated January 6, 2021, from documents produced to the Minority Staff of the Committee on House Administration from the House Sergeant at Arms on January 28, 2022.

453. *Priority – Breach on West Front (update)*, Email dated January 6, 2021, from documents produced to the Minority Staff of the Committee on House Administration from the House Sergeant at Arms on January 28, 2022.

454. *Protestors*, Email dated January 6, 2021, from documents produced to the Minority Staff of the Committee on House Administration from the House Sergeant at Arms on January 28, 2022.

455. *Large breach east front*, Email dated January 6, 2021, from documents produced to the Minority Staff of the Committee on House Administration from the House Sergeant at Arms on January 28, 2022.

456. Phone records from documents produced to the Minority Staff of the Committee on House Administration from the House Sergeant at Arms on January 28, 2022.

457. Phone records from documents produced to the Minority Staff of the Committee on House Administration from the House Sergeant at Arms on January 28, 2022.

458. *Shelter in Place – CHOB, LHOB RHOB*, Email dated January 6, 2021, from documents produced to the Minority Staff of the Committee on House Administration from the House Sergeant at Arms on January 28, 2022.

459. *Priority – Breach on West Front (update)*, Email dated January 6, 2021, from documents produced to the Minority Staff of the Committee on House Administration from the House Sergeant at Arms on January 28, 2022.

460. Phone records from documents produced to the Minority Staff of the Committee on House Administration from the House Sergeant at Arms on January 28, 2022.

461. Phone records from documents produced to the Minority Staff of the Committee on House Administration from the House Sergeant at Arms on January 28, 2022.

462. *2nd Breach – East Front*, Email dated January 6, 2021, from documents produced to the Minority Staff of the Committee on House Administration from the House Sergeant at Arms on January 28, 2022.

ENDNOTES

463. *Rotunda Door*, Email dated January 6, 2021, from documents produced to the Minority Staff of the Committee on House Administration from the House Sergeant at Arms on January 28, 2022.

464. *LOCKDOWN - entire campus*, Email dated January 6, 2021, from documents produced to the Minority Staff of the Committee on House Administration from the House Sergeant at Arms on January 28, 2022.

465. Phone records from documents produced to the Minority Staff of the Committee on House Administration from the House Sergeant at Arms on January 28, 2022.

466. Text Message dated January 6, 2021, from documents produced to the Minority Staff of the Committee on House Administration from the House Sergeant at Arms on January 28, 2022.

467. Phone records from documents produced to the Minority Staff of the Committee on House Administration from the House Sergeant at Arms on January 28, 2022.

468. *[Redacted]*, Email dated January 6, 2021, from documents produced to the Minority Staff of the Committee on House Administration from the House Sergeant at Arms on January 28, 2022.

469. Phone records from documents produced to the Minority Staff of the Committee on House Administration from the House Sergeant at Arms on January 28, 2022.

470. *Capitol breached, exterior perimeter compromised*, Email dated January 6, 2021, from documents produced to the Minority Staff of the Committee on House Administration from the House Sergeant at Arms on January 28, 2022.

471. Phone records from documents produced to the Minority Staff of the Committee on House Administration from the House Sergeant at Arms on January 28, 2022.

472. Phone records from documents produced to the Minority Staff of the Committee on House Administration from the House Sergeant at Arms on January 28, 2022.

473. *Chamber Evacuation*, Email dated January 6, 2021, from documents produced to the Minority Staff of the Committee on House Administration from the House Sergeant at Arms on January 28, 2022.

474. Phone records from documents produced to the Minority Staff of the Committee on House Administration from the House Sergeant at Arms on January 28, 2022.

475. *House Chamber - compromised*, Email dated January 6, 2021, from documents produced to the Minority Staff of the Committee on House Administration from the House Sergeant at Arms on January 28, 2022.

476. Phone records from documents produced to the Minority Staff of the Committee on House Administration from the House Sergeant at Arms on January 28, 2022.

ENDNOTES

477. *SHOTS FIRED – HOUSE FLOOR*, Email dated January 6, 2021, from documents produced to the Minority Staff of the Committee on House Administration from the House Sergeant at Arms on January 28, 2022.

478. Phone records from documents produced to the Minority Staff of the Committee on House Administration from the House Sergeant at Arms on January 28, 2022.

479. *Reports of officer down*, Email dated January 6, 2021, from documents produced to the Minority Staff of the Committee on House Administration from the House Sergeant at Arms on January 28, 2022.

480. Phone records from documents produced to the Minority Staff of the Committee on House Administration from the House Sergeant at Arms on January 28, 2022.

481. Phone records from documents produced to the Minority Staff of the Committee on House Administration from the House Sergeant at Arms on January 28, 2022.

482. Phone records from documents produced to the Minority Staff of the Committee on House Administration from the House Sergeant at Arms on January 28, 2022.

483. Phone records from documents produced to the Minority Staff of the Committee on House Administration from the House Sergeant at Arms on January 28, 2022.

484. Text Message dated January 6, 2021, from documents produced to the Minority Staff of the Committee on House Administration from the House Sergeant at Arms on January 28, 2022.

485. Phone records from documents produced to the Minority Staff of the Committee on House Administration from the House Sergeant at Arms on January 28, 2022.

486. Phone records from documents produced to the Minority Staff of the Committee on House Administration from the House Sergeant at Arms on January 28, 2022.

487. Phone records from documents produced to the Minority Staff of the Committee on House Administration from the House Sergeant at Arms on January 28, 2022.

488. Phone records from documents produced to the Minority Staff of the Committee on House Administration from the House Sergeant at Arms on January 28, 2022.

489. Phone records from documents produced to the Minority Staff of the Committee on House Administration from the House Sergeant at Arms on January 28, 2022.

490. Phone records from documents produced to the Minority Staff of the Committee on House Administration from the House Sergeant at Arms on January 28, 2022.

491. Phone records from documents produced to the Minority Staff of the Committee on House Administration from the House Sergeant at Arms on January 28, 2022.

ENDNOTES

492. Phone records from documents produced to the Minority Staff of the Committee on House Administration from the House Sergeant at Arms on January 28, 2022.

493. Phone records from documents produced to the Minority Staff of the Committee on House Administration from the House Sergeant at Arms on January 28, 2022.

494. Phone records from documents produced to the Minority Staff of the Committee on House Administration from the House Sergeant at Arms on January 28, 2022.

495. *CNN Report*, Email dated January 6, 2021, from documents produced to the Minority Staff of the Committee on House Administration from the House Sergeant at Arms on January 28, 2022.

496. *VIDEO & Immediate investigation*, Email dated January 6, 2021, from documents produced to the Minority Staff of the Committee on House Administration from the House Sergeant at Arms on January 28, 2022.

497. Phone records from documents produced to the Minority Staff of the Committee on House Administration from the House Sergeant at Arms on January 28, 2022.

498. Phone records from documents produced to the Minority Staff of the Committee on House Administration from the House Sergeant at Arms on January 28, 2022.

499. Phone records from documents produced to the Minority Staff of the Committee on House Administration from the House Sergeant at Arms on January 28, 2022.

500. Text Message dated January 6, 2021, from documents produced to the Minority Staff of the Committee on House Administration from the House Sergeant at Arms on January 28, 2022.

501. Text Message dated January 6, 2021, from documents produced to the Minority Staff of the Committee on House Administration from the House Sergeant at Arms on January 28, 2022.

502. *Update from Waldow*, Email dated January 6, 2021, from documents produced to the Minority Staff of the Committee on House Administration from the House Sergeant at Arms on January 28, 2022.

503. Phone records from documents produced to the Minority Staff of the Committee on House Administration from the House Sergeant at Arms on January 28, 2022.

504. Phone records from documents produced to the Minority Staff of the Committee on House Administration from the House Sergeant at Arms on January 28, 2022.

505. Phone records from documents produced to the Minority Staff of the Committee on House Administration from the House Sergeant at Arms on January 28, 2022.

506. *Update: West Front*, Email dated January 6, 2021, from documents produced to the Minority Staff of the Committee on House Administration from the House Sergeant at Arms on January 28, 2022.

ENDNOTES

507. Phone records from documents produced to the Minority Staff of the Committee on House Administration from the House Sergeant at Arms on January 28, 2022.

508. Text Message dated January 6, 2021, from documents produced to the Minority Staff of the Committee on House Administration from the House Sergeant at Arms on January 28, 2022.

509. Phone records from documents produced to the Minority Staff of the Committee on House Administration from the House Sergeant at Arms on January 28, 2022.

510. Phone records from documents produced to the Minority Staff of the Committee on House Administration from the House Sergeant at Arms on January 28, 2022.

511. Text Message dated January 6, 2021, from documents produced to the Minority Staff of the Committee on House Administration from the House Sergeant at Arms on January 28, 2022.

512. Phone records from documents produced to the Minority Staff of the Committee on House Administration from the House Sergeant at Arms on January 28, 2022.

513. Phone records from documents produced to the Minority Staff of the Committee on House Administration from the House Sergeant at Arms on January 28, 2022.

514. *Status Brief*, Email dated January 6, 2021, from documents produced to the Minority Staff of the Committee on House Administration from the House Sergeant at Arms on January 28, 2022.

515. Phone records from documents produced to the Minority Staff of the Committee on House Administration from the House Sergeant at Arms on January 28, 2022.

516. Phone records from documents produced to the Minority Staff of the Committee on House Administration from the House Sergeant at Arms on January 28, 2022.

517. Phone records from documents produced to the Minority Staff of the Committee on House Administration from the House Sergeant at Arms on January 28, 2022.

518. Phone records from documents produced to the Minority Staff of the Committee on House Administration from the House Sergeant at Arms on January 28, 2022.

519. Text Message dated January 6, 2021, from documents produced to the Minority Staff of the Committee on House Administration from the House Sergeant at Arms on January 28, 2022.

520. Exterior sweeps, Email dated January 6, 2021, from documents produced to the Minority Staff of the Committee on House Administration from the House Sergeant at Arms on January 28, 2022.

ENDNOTES

521. Phone records from documents produced to the Minority Staff of the Committee on House Administration from the House Sergeant at Arms on January 28, 2022.

522. Phone records from documents produced to the Minority Staff of the Committee on House Administration from the House Sergeant at Arms on January 28, 2022.

523. Phone records from documents produced to the Minority Staff of the Committee on House Administration from the House Sergeant at Arms on January 28, 2022.

524. Phone records from documents produced to the Minority Staff of the Committee on House Administration from the House Sergeant at Arms on January 28, 2022.

525. Phone records from documents produced to the Minority Staff of the Committee on House Administration from the House Sergeant at Arms on January 28, 2022.

526. *(no subject)*, Email dated January 6, 2021, from documents produced to the Minority Staff of the Committee on House Administration from the House Sergeant at Arms on January 28, 2022.

527. *Possible Message to Reconvene*, Email dated January 6, 2021, from documents produced to the Minority Staff of the Committee on House Administration from the House Sergeant at Arms on January 28, 2022.

528. Phone records from documents produced to the Minority Staff of the Committee on House Administration from the House Sergeant at Arms on January 28, 2022.

529. Phone records from documents produced to the Minority Staff of the Committee on House Administration from the House Sergeant at Arms on January 28, 2022.

530. *Capitol Is Secure*, Email dated January 6, 2021, from documents produced to the Minority Staff of the Committee on House Administration from the House Sergeant at Arms on January 28, 2022.

531. *Re: Capitol Is Secure*, Email dated January 6, 2021, from documents produced to the Minority Staff of the Committee on House Administration from the House Sergeant at Arms on January 28, 2022.

532. Phone records from documents produced to the Minority Staff of the Committee on House Administration from the House Sergeant at Arms on January 28, 2022.

533. Phone records from documents produced to the Minority Staff of the Committee on House Administration from the House Sergeant at Arms on January 28, 2022.

534. Phone records from documents produced to the Minority Staff of the Committee on House Administration from the House Sergeant at Arms on January 28, 2022.

535. Text Message dated January 6, 2021, from documents produced to the Minority Staff of the Committee on House Administration from the House Sergeant at Arms on January 28, 2022.

ENDNOTES

536. *Fwd: Capitol Police firings imminent after 'attempted coup,' top appropriator warns*, Email dated January 6, 2021, from documents produced to the Minority Staff of the Committee on House Administration from the House Sergeant at Arms on January 28, 2022.

537. *Approval Needed – Emergency Board Orders*, Email dated January 6, 2021, from documents produced to the Minority Staff of the Committee on House Administration from the House Sergeant at Arms on January 28, 2022.

538. Text Message dated January 6, 2021, from documents produced to the Minority Staff of the Committee on House Administration from the House Sergeant at Arms on January 28, 2022.

539. Phone records from documents produced to the Minority Staff of the Committee on House Administration from the House Sergeant at Arms on January 28, 2022.

540. *RE: Approval Needed – Emergency Board Orders*, Email dated January 6, 2021, from documents produced to the Minority Staff of the Committee on House Administration from the House Sergeant at Arms on January 28, 2022.

541. *Re: Approval Needed – Emergency Board Orders*, Email dated January 6, 2021, from documents produced to the Minority Staff of the Committee on House Administration from the House Sergeant at Arms on January 28, 2022.

542. *Re: Approval Needed – Emergency Board Orders*, Email dated January 6, 2021, from documents produced to the Minority Staff of the Committee on House Administration from the House Sergeant at Arms on January 28, 2022.

543. Phone records from documents produced to the Minority Staff of the Committee on House Administration from the House Sergeant at Arms on January 28, 2022.

544. *(no subject)*, Email dated January 6, 2021, from documents produced to the Minority Staff of the Committee on House Administration from the House Sergeant at Arms on January 28, 2022.

545. *Re:*, Email dated January 6, 2021, from documents produced to the Minority Staff of the Committee on House Administration from the House Sergeant at Arms on January 28, 2022.

546. *Fwd:*, Email dated January 6, 2021, from documents produced to the Minority Staff of the Committee on House Administration from the House Sergeant at Arms on January 28, 2022.

547. *STATEMENT – USCP Statement – Events of January 6 2021 V1.docx*, Email dated January 7, 2021, from documents produced to the Minority Staff of the Committee on House Administration from the House Sergeant at Arms on January 28, 2022.

ENDNOTES

548. *Fwd: Disaster Assessment*, Email dated January 7, 2021, from documents produced to the Minority Staff of the Committee on House Administration from the House Sergeant at Arms on January 28, 2022.

549. *ID Checks Today*, Email dated January 7, 2021, from documents produced to the Minority Staff of the Committee on House Administration from the House Sergeant at Arms on January 28, 2022.

550. *TSA*, Email dated January 7, 2021, from documents produced to the Minority Staff of the Committee on House Administration from the House Sergeant at Arms on January 28, 2022.

551. *USCP Press Release for January 6, 2021 Events*, Email dated January 7, 2021, from documents produced to the Minority Staff of the Committee on House Administration from the House Sergeant at Arms on January 28, 2022.

552. *Arrest numbers*, Email dated January 7, 2021, from documents produced to the Minority Staff of the Committee on House Administration from the House Sergeant at Arms on January 28, 2022.

553. *Fwd: ID Checks Today*, Email dated January 7, 2021, from documents produced to the Minority Staff of the Committee on House Administration from the House Sergeant at Arms on January 28, 2022.

554. *STAND STRONG, SIR*, Email dated January 7, 2021, from documents produced to the Minority Staff of the Committee on House Administration from the House Sergeant at Arms on January 28, 2022.

555. *Security Update & Door Access*, Email dated January 7, 2021, from documents produced to the Minority Staff of the Committee on House Administration from the House Sergeant at Arms on January 28, 2022.

556. Text Message dated January 7, 2021, from documents produced to the Minority Staff of the Committee on House Administration from the House Sergeant at Arms on January 28, 2022.

557. Text Message dated January 7, 2021, from documents produced to the Minority Staff of the Committee on House Administration from the House Sergeant at Arms on January 28, 2022.

558. Text Message dated January 7, 2021, from documents produced to the Minority Staff of the Committee on House Administration from the House Sergeant at Arms on January 28, 2022.

559. Text Message dated January 8, 2021, from documents produced to the Minority Staff of the Committee on House Administration from the House Sergeant at Arms on January 28, 2022.

ENDNOTES

560. Text Message dated January 8, 2021, from documents produced to the Minority Staff of the Committee on House Administration from the House Sergeant at Arms on January 28, 2022.

561. Text Message dated January 10, 2021, from documents produced to the Minority Staff of the Committee on House Administration from the House Sergeant at Arms on January 28, 2022.

562. Text Message dated January 10, 2021, from documents produced to the Minority Staff of the Committee on House Administration from the House Sergeant at Arms on January 28, 2022.

563. Text Message dated January 13, 2021, from documents produced to the Minority Staff of the Committee on House Administration from the House Sergeant at Arms on January 28, 2022.

564. This organizational chart is not an exhaustive chart of all security entities, only those relevant to this report. The sources for this chart include a chart provided to the Minority Staff of the Committee on House Administration by the U.S. Capitol Police and a chart found in the March 7, 2022, GAO report, "Capitol Attack: Additional Actions Needed to Better Prepare Capitol Police Officers for Violent Demonstrations." The Chief of Police is a non-voting member of the Board; Gov't Accountability Office, GAO-22-104829, Capitol Attack Additional Actions Needed to Better Prepare Capitol Police Officers for Violent Demonstrations (2022), https://www.gao.gov/assets/gao-22-104829.pdf

www.ingramcontent.com/pod-product-compliance
Lightning Source LLC
Chambersburg PA
CBHW080601270326
41928CB00038B/3216